INSTRUMENTO DE OBSERVACIÓN

DE LOS LOGROS DE LA LECTO-ESCRITURA INICIAL

SPANISH RECONSTRUCTION OF
An Observation Survey
A BILINGUAL TEXT

INSTRUMENTO DE OBSERVACIÓN

DE LOS LOGROS DE LA LECTO-ESCRITURA INICIAL

Kathy Escamilla, Ana María Andrade
Amelia G. M. Basurto, Olivia A. Ruiz

in collaboration with
Marie M. Clay

HEINEMANN • PORTSMOUTH, NH

Heinemann

361 Hanover Street
Portsmouth, NH 03801-3912

Offices and agents throughout the world

The authors and publisher wish to thank those who have generously given permission to reprint borrowed material:
Page 43: From *La Gallinita Roja* illustrated by Lucinda McQueen, translated by Elva R. Lopez. Illustration copyright © 1985 by Lucinda McQueen, translation copyright © 1987 by Scholastic Inc. Reprinted by permission of Scholastic Inc.

Library of Congress Cataloging-in-Publication Data

Instrumento de observación de los logros de la lecto-escritura inicial
: a bilingual text / Kathy Escamilla . . . [et al.] ; in collaboration
with Marie M. Clay.
    p.   cm.
''Spanish reconstruction of An observation survey''—CIP t.p.
Includes bibliographical references (p. 124) and index.
ISBN 0-435-08858-0
1. Reading (Primary)—New Zealand.   2. Reading (Primary)—New
Zealand—Ability testing.   3. Spanish language—Composition and
exercises—Study and teaching (Primary)—New Zealand.   4. Spanish
language—Composition and exercises—New Zealand—Ability testing.
5. Observation (Educational method)   6. Education, Bilingual—New
Zealand.   I. Escamilla, Kathy.   II. Clay, Marie M. An observation survey.
LB1525.I57   1995
372.4049—dc20   95-31356
                                                                                          CIP

Editor: Leigh Peake
Production: Vicki Kasabian
Cover design: Darci Mehall

Printed in the United States of America on acid-free paper
Docutech T & C 2009

CONTENTS

ACKNOWLEDGMENTS

This publication emerged from the need to disseminate the Spanish reconstruction of the Observation Survey to teachers working with emergent Spanish readers in the United States. We would like to take this opportunity to acknowledge Dr. Marie Clay for her willingness to support this project and for providing direction in the development of *EL INSTRUMENTO DE OBSERVACIÓN*.

We would also like to recognize the following sites and their staffs who provided support and their expertise to this project.

California State University, San Bernardino, San Bernardino, California
Carrollton-Farmers Branch Independent School District, Carrollton, Texas
Chicago Public Schools
Los Angeles County Department of Education
McAllen Independent School District, McAllen, Texas
National Louis University, Chicago, Illinois

Northside Independent School District, San Antonio, Texas
Office of Educational Research and Improvement, Washington, D.C.
Philip Sheridan Public School, Chicago, Illinois
Texas Woman's University, Denton, Texas
Tucson Unified School District
University of Colorado, Denver, Denver, Colorado

Special thanks to Lydia García for providing us with translations and guidance and Frank Valenzuela for his patience and for creating wonderful graphics.

INTRODUCTION

Kathy Escamilla
Ana María Andrade
Amelia G. M. Basurto
Olivia A. Ruiz

The work of Dr. Marie Clay has steadily gained stature and recognition throughout the world. The power of systematic observation is now well documented as a vehicle for informing teachers and improving instruction when English is used as the medium of instruction and observation. The success of this work has raised the question of the potential of these same observational tasks when developed and applied in languages other than English.

This book represents six years of work in the development and implementation of Clay's original observation tasks in Spanish, as well as implementation of early intervention literacy programs in Spanish. The work presented in this book was developed and field tested with Spanish-speaking students living and attending school in the United States. Spanish, in this context, is the language most often spoken and best understood by these children. However, since they reside in the United States, they come into contact every day with English language and print. As such, they are not simply Spanish-speaking children, they are two-language children. Great consideration was given in the development of this work to issues raised when two languages and cultures come into contact. The context is bilingual and biliterate, not simply a work re-created from English to Spanish. This work, then, should be viewed as a beginning effort to observe and begin to address literacy development in two-language children.

Aside from the above, the authors believe that *El Instrumento de Observación* (Spanish Observation Survey) presented in this book could also be used effectively in Spanish-speaking countries with little modification.

Since the work was developed for use in the United States, the explanations of theoretical concepts, procedures used in creating the Spanish Observation Tasks, research results, and directions to the teachers are all presented in English. The observation tasks, examples of student responses to these tasks, and directions for administering these tasks to students are all written in Spanish. Response and recording sheets for running records are written both in Spanish and English. Response and recording sheets for all other tasks are written in Spanish only.

The authors felt that this format would enable the document to be understood by the larger community of professional educators in the United States involved in literacy instruction with students who speak languages other than English. This community includes professional educators who are bilingual and biliterate as well as those who are not bilingual but are in positions where daily they interact with and make instructional decisions about students who do not speak English. The observation survey itself, however, is designed to be used by bilingual/biliterate teachers who have been fully prepared to be bilingual education teachers and have also been trained in the administration and scoring of *El Instrumento de Observación* (Spanish Observation Survey).

As a result of our work in developing and implementing Clay's observational tasks in Spanish, we feel that systematic observation has the same potential for improving literacy instruction in Spanish that it does in English. We echo Clay's belief that *information that is gathered in systematic observation reduces our uncertainties and improves our instruction.*

The theoretical framework that guided the development of this book comes from the work of Clay as well as the field of bilingual education. As such, it has been organized into four major sections. Section I (Chapters 1–3) is a reprint of the original work of Marie Clay that discusses in detail her thirty years of work related to systematic observation of reading behaviors and the need for early intervention to detect and correct reading difficulties. Since the work is a reprint of Clay's original work, it is written in the first person (Clay's voice).

Section II (Chapters 4–5) presents a discussion of the rationale for early intervention programs in Spanish for Spanish-speaking students in bilingual education programs in the United States. Chapter 4 outlines the theoretical framework and research base for the use of native language programs. Chapter 5 presents a detailed discussion of the reconstruction of the English Observation Survey into Spanish. The word reconstruction is a key term used throughout this book to illustrate that *El Instrumento de Observación*, as the survey has been titled in Spanish, is **not** a literal translation of Clay's work nor is it an equivalent. Rather, it is a conceptual re-creation of the work of Clay from English to Spanish that further considers how children who come into contact with two languages use those two languages to make sense of their world. Documentation and discussion of conceptual issues that were considered and critical decisions that were made with regard to this reconstruction are included in Chapter 5.

Section III (Chapters 6–8) presents the work on the reconstruction of the English Observation Survey into *El Instrumento de Observación* to date. Chapter 6 discusses the taking of running records with Spanish-speaking children and Spanish texts. Included in this chapter are conventions for scoring running records taken in Spanish.

Chapter 7 discusses other observation tasks that have been developed in Spanish and includes administration and scoring procedures. Included in this chapter are research results related to validity and reliability tests conducted on all of the Spanish observation tasks. Chapter 8 provides direction for summarizing the observation results and ways in which teachers can use the results of the types of observations for improving Spanish reading instruction.

Section IV (Chapter 9) discusses the uses of observation tasks such as this one and Clay's original work to inform both teachers and the educational system about children's progress and their needs in the acquisition of early literacy.

Collectively, this work is meant to expand the knowledge base of bilingual education teachers and others who are working with Spanish-speaking students in a way that enables them to be better observers of children's literacy behaviors, thereby improving instruction for this group of children. This work is important since Spanish-speaking children constitute the fastest growing group of school-aged children in the United States. Additionally, it is hoped that this book will also help advance the knowledge base related to the implementation of programs of bilingual education in the United States.

SECTION I

INTRODUCTION AND THEORETICAL FRAMEWORK

1 OBSERVING CHANGE IN EARLY LITERACY BEHAVIOURS

Marie Clay

AN INTRODUCTION TO SYSTEMATIC OBSERVATION

Observation in classrooms

Observation of what goes on in classrooms has uncovered differences in time allocations which suggest that high progress children get more opportunities to learn than low progress children. Studies have produced evidence of how the successful children tend to get better and better, drawing away from the average or below average children whose progress proceeds at an apparently slower rate. However, this slow rate of learning can occur because children do not get the kinds of help they need to learn at faster rates.

Observing individual progress

If we attend to individual children as they work, and if we focus on the progressions in learning that occur over time, such observations can provide feedback to our instruction. Observations which lead us to modify our instruction are particularly appropriate in the formative stages of new learning, as in beginning reading, beginning writing and beginning mathematics.

I have tried to observe individual children at work, reading and writing, and to capture evidence of the progress that they make. Science is based on systematic observation of phenomena under known conditions. Physicists or chemists in laboratories, botanists and zoologists in the field, and behavioural scientists in psychology, sociology, linguistics and cultural anthropology all use observation to get research data. Despite some lingering mistrust of observation in educational research, it is becoming more acceptable to use direct observation as a method for data collection, particularly in the years of early childhood education (Genishi 1982).

With good reason educators have relied on systematic testing rather than systematic observation of learning. The measurement theories that are used to guide test construction and research analyses lead to better interpretations of test and examination results. But as we have improved our testing strategies we have placed undue emphasis on testing to the point where we can deprive teachers and administrators of valuable information about learners and their learning. There is a seductive efficiency about final assessment scores. Yet a funny thing happens on the way to those final assessments: day-to-day learning takes place. In education, we need to pay more attention to the evaluation of learners who are on the way to those final assessments. One of the things that a class teacher needs to know is what occurs over time for the individual learner in a particular classroom programme.

We do need research endeavour which looks for explanations of what causes what, or what conditions bring about differences, and such questions call for the use of a variety of research paradigms, but for effective instruction we also need answers to two basic questions: 'What typically occurs for children like those I teach as learning takes place over the school year?' and 'How is this individual child changing over time in relation to what typically occurs?' Teachers who have answers to these questions will be more responsive to the daily learning of their pupils and will deliver more appropriate feedback.

In developmental psychology young children were always studied by direct observation. Studies of how children learn to speak have been exciting, and so have the more recent studies of young children learning to read and write. But teachers must go beyond reactions like 'Ooh! Ah!', or 'I am surprised!' and 'Isn't that cute!' and try to understand what is happening and why it is happening.

Measuring outcomes

Historically, most assessment has been directed to the outcomes of instruction. We wait until the end of the instruction sequence before we assess. We

- monitor for national performance
- assess the effectiveness of schools
- assess the effectiveness of teachers
- assess primary school outcome achievements
- assess secondary school outcome achievements.

When we measure the outcomes of teaching with important tests the instruction of the learners is already over. The test score is, in legal terms, after the fact. It is almost too late to change the fate of the students because of what we find out. The opportunity has gone.

We do not have to test all children to assess educational standards at the national, state, or district level; we can use sampling methods to get information on standards in the same way that we take public opinion polls. We do not need to test every child to know whether the school system is producing satisfactory outcomes. And in many countries there is some agreement that this measurement of the education system can be done best from the age of nine years and upwards.

Measures of outcome tell us where the achievement levels of the education system lie. They do not tell us what brought about those achievement levels. We do not know from the assessments how the high achievement levels were obtained, or why the low achievement levels occurred. If we try to use those results to improve instruction

- we can only guess how to change our teaching
- we can only guess how to change our policies
- we can only guess what factors produced the scores.

Measuring abilities

Measurement theory has allowed us to measure the abilities of individual learners—intelligence, language skills, auditory and visual perception, and so on. When we measure these things we *predict* how well an individual student might learn in our programmes. This type of testing is usually done before instruction and it has resulted in children being grouped according to estimated abilities.

Even when we give these tests to individuals we score them according to what we know happens to groups of children. We predict for individuals from *group* data, not from individual data. We use norms, or average scores for children of the same age. Such predictions are often wrong for individual children.

If teachers do use outcome tests and ability scores, and many will be required to do so, they should be aware that every expectation they hold of what a child can and cannot learn should be mistrusted, in the sense of holding a tentative hypothesis that can be revised. For if we give the learner particular opportunities and the right learning conditions, that learner might prove the test's predictions to be wrong. Teachers should always leave room to be surprised by individual children.

Every test score has some error of measurement attached to it; there is error in group scores, and error in individual scores. We should keep an open mind on what is possible for the individual child to achieve. We have in the past sometimes made assumptions about children that closed the possibility of their learning more.

When our predictions are wrong for individual children, education practices tend to deprive those children of opportunities to learn. We keep them away from certain challenges (we keep them out of school, or we hold them back to repeat the same class with the same curriculum, or we give them less to learn, or we give them drastically simplified tasks).

Assessments that guide our teaching

Effective teaching calls for a third kind of assessment designed to record how the child works on tasks and to inform teaching as it occurs. To use the metaphor of a football game, you do not improve the play of a team by looking at the outcome score. The coach must look closely at how the team is playing the game and help them to change the moves or strategies that produce a better final score.

When the class teacher observes how individual children are problem-solving, it makes a difference to what happens in classrooms. It is particularly useful in three kinds of situations:

- for young children up to eight years of age
- at the introduction of new areas of learning
- when the activity being learned is complex.

Classroom teachers can observe students as they construct responses by moving among them while they work. They can observe how individuals change over time by keeping good records. And they can allow children to take different learning paths to the same outcomes because they are clearly aware of the learning that is occurring.

Such teachers are like craftsmen, monitoring how their products take shape. Think of the painter or potter adjusting the light, shade, colour, shape or texture of a product in formation. Or we could think of the violinist in the orchestra who knows that one of his strings is slipping off pitch. He takes an opportunity during a pause in the performance to avert disaster by tightening the string. He would not wait for the critic's review of the performance in the morning paper, saying one violin was out of tune! Skilled craftspeople fine-tune the ongoing construction or performance. Teachers should work in this way.

To improve teaching teachers need to observe children's responses during literacy instruction

* for competencies and confusions
* for strengths and weaknesses
* for the processes and strategies used
* for evidence of what the child already understands.

Observing oral language

Early childhood education has used observations of what children can do because little children often cannot put into words what they are doing or thinking.

In the past 25 years, studies of how children learn to speak have been exciting. In the 1960s researchers went into homes to observe children learning language and record its use as it occurred in natural settings. They followed the progress of particular children as they developed and their language changed. They studied what actually occurred, making precise records, and they did not depend on tests or on recollections of what occurred (Brown 1973, Paley 1981, Wells 1986).

Interest shifted from an early focus on the structures of language to meaning. In the 1970s this led us to study the effects of the contexts in which language occurs. The young child's language is so related to the things he is talking about that you can have trouble understanding him unless you also know about the things he refers to. We became more sensitive to the ways in which we change our language according to the place we are in, and who we are talking to. We learned more about the ways in which the languages of the homes differ, more about dialects and more about the complexities of bilingual learning.

Attention moved to the detailed study of interactions between mothers and children, teachers and children, children and children. As a result of all this recording of naturally occurring behaviour we now know a great deal about the ways in which the contexts of language interactions facilitate or constrain the development of language in children. We know that entry into formal education settings such as schools reduces children's opportunities for talking, and that some types of programmes prevent children from using the excellent and efficient ways of learning language which they used before they came to school (Cazden 1988).

Observing emerging literacy

There have been many exciting observational studies of children's writing since the 1970s. The young child has emerged as an active participant in the process of becoming a writer. To take only one illustration, the studies of Mexican and Argentinean children by Ferreiro and Teberosky (1982) described the fascinating shifts occurring well before children begin to use the alphabetical principle of letter-sound relationships, which we commonly think of as the beginning of writing. These preschool children were making discoveries about writing, constructing the writing system and making it their own. The observation of early writing behaviours has taken us forward in great leaps since 1975.

Many observers discovered that preschool children explore the detail of print in their environment, on signs, cereal packets and television advertisements. They develop concepts about books, newspapers and messages, and what it is to read these. Case studies over long periods of time show how children change over time and how more advanced concepts emerge out of earlier understandings.

Preschool children already know something about the world of print from their environments. This leads them to form primitive hypotheses about letters, words or messages both printed and handwritten. It is a widely held view that learning to read and write in school will be easier for the child with rich preschool literacy experiences than it is for the child who has had few opportunities for such learning.

We have learned of these things mainly through research which has used observation rather than experimentation as its method. When we become neutral observers and watch children at work in systematic and repeatable ways we begin to uncover some of our own assumptions and notice how wrong these can sometimes be.

Observing school entrants

Systematic observation of school entrants has distinct advantages over readiness testing. At entry to school children have been learning for five to six years, since they were born. They are all ready to learn more than they already know. Why do schools and educators find this so difficult to understand? Teachers must find out what children already know, and take them from where they are to somewhere else.

When we give a 'readiness test' to a new school entrant we are trying to predict school progress from what a child already knows (see Measuring abilities, page 6). We are merely asking 'Are you ready for my programme?' Readiness tests divide children into a competent group ready to learn on a particular programme and a problem group supposedly not ready to learn. On the other hand, observations which record what learners already know about emerging literacy eliminate the problem group. *They are all ready to learn something*, but are starting from different places.

Suppose we observe the literacy behaviours of a group of new school entrants. Some know a little about reading and writing and others know very little. Those who know very little may have paid almost no attention to print in their preschool years because they had little opportunity or encouragement, or no incentive or interest. Or perhaps some adults around them tried to teach them and the children found the tasks very confusing and so withdrew their effort to learn. Undoubtedly, what the young child knows about literacy when he or she enters school is not a matter of competency unfolding from within, for in an oral culture where literacy does not exist, no such behaviour unfolds. It is a matter of opportunities to learn about a very arbitrary symbol system. There will be individual differences for other reasons but the one aspect of this development that we can influence and foster is in the area of appropriate opportunities to learn. That usually means providing a responsive environment within which the child can explore and negotiate meanings.

When children enter school we need to observe what they know and can do, and build on that foundation whether it is rich or meager.

The New Zealand teachers I worked with in various research projects did observe children when they entered school and taught to expand the various competencies that children already had. They taught in ways that introduced children to print in reading and in writing activities so that they could learn more than they already knew. They gave more help and more attention to the children who knew the least, making up for missed opportunities to learn.

The observation tasks used in this Survey are *not* readiness tests which sort children into who is ready to face literacy learning and who is not. In particular the Concepts About Print (CAP) task is not a readiness test because it only samples one dimension of a child's preparation for formal instruction. However, '. . . in the United States . . . the CAP tests have tended to be used in kindergarten in much the same way that readiness tests are often used' (Stallman and Pearson 1990). While those authors look to the construction of better commercially available tests of readiness, I strongly support the abandonment of the readiness concept in its old form. All children are ready to learn; it is the teachers who need to know how to create appropriate instruction for where each child is. To do this effectively they need to observe a wide range of literacy behaviours throughout the first years of school. (See also Clay 1991, p. 19.)

My theoretical analysis of beginning reading and writing tells me that children have to extend their knowledge along each of several different dimensions of learning as they approach formal literacy instruction. At the same time they have to learn how to relate learning in any one of these areas (say letter learning) to learning in any other (say messages and meanings). Along each of these dimensions more learning has to occur. It does not happen in an orderly way. It is not the same for all children. Each learner starts with what he or she already knows and uses that to support what has to be learnt next.

To become observers of the early stages of literacy learning teachers will have to give up looking for a single, short assessment test for the acquisition stages of reading and writing. Children move into reading by different tracks and early assessments must be wide-ranging. If there is a single task that stands up better than any other it is the running record of text reading. This is a neutral observation task, capable of use in any system of reading, and recording progress on whatever gradient of text difficulty has been adopted by the education system. (See pages 39–67; also Johnston 1992).

Standardised tests do not measure slow progress well

It is difficult to design a good reading assessment instrument which can be used close to the onset of instruction. Standardised tests sample from all behaviours and they do not discriminate well until considerable progress has been made by many of the children (Clay 1991, page 204). Yet teachers can identify the children making slow progress before standardised tests can do this effectively. In my own research 20 to 25 percent of beginning readers were showing some confusions and difficulties one year to 18 months before good assessments could be obtained by standardised tests of reading for children in the tail end of the distribution of test scores. We should try to use systematic observation by teachers as one way to achieve early identification of children who need supplementary help.

I have come to place less emphasis on assessments which yield an age or grade level score in the first years of school. A programme of assessment will give me checkpoints on the general level of performance of children but I would want to have, in addition, records of progress on individual children—where they were at various points during the year, what products they could produce and what processes they could control on what texts.

To be acceptable as evidence of children's progress observational data would have to be as reliable as test data. Running records have shown high reliability, with scores for accuracy and error having reliability of 0.90. Observers find self-correction behaviour harder to agree upon and the reliability can drop to 0.70.

Running records of text reading have face and content validity. You cannot get closer to the valid measure of oral reading than to be able to say the child can read the book you want him to be reading at this or that level with this or that kind of processing behaviour. Little or nothing is inferred. You can count the number of correct words to get an accuracy score. The record does not give a measure of comprehension but you can tell from the child's responses to the story and from the analysis of error and self-correction behaviour how well the child works for meaning. And you can gauge his understanding of the story in the discussion you have with him about the story. You do not get a score on letters known, but you can see whether the child uses letter knowledge on the run in his reading.

In summary, standardised tests are indirect ways of observing children's progress. They are suitable for reporting the behaviours of groups but cannot compare with the observation of learners at work for providing the information needed to design sound instruction.

Systematic observation

Educators have done a great deal of systematic testing and relatively little systematic observation of learning. One could argue that educators need to give most of their attention to the systematic observation of learners who are on the way to those final scores on tests.

Systematic observations have four characteristics in common with good measurement instruments. They provide:

- a standard task
- a standard way of setting up the task (administration)
- ways of knowing when we can rely on our observations and make reliable comparisons
- a task that is like a real world task as a guarantee that the observations will relate to what the child is likely to do in the real world (for this establishes the validity of the observation).

The standard task and administration provide sound measurement conditions. Otherwise we would be evaluating with a piece of elastic instead of using an instrument that behaves in the same way on every occasion. Two measurements with a piece of elastic cannot be compared; and comparability is often important not only at the national, state and district level but also at the individual level. For we often want to compare a student on two of his own performances. A standard task, which is administered and scored in a standard way, gives one kind of guarantee of reliability in comparisons.

Not all of our observations have to be on standard tasks but those used to demonstrate change over time should be. The problem with observations is that they can have many sources of error. One of these sources of 'error' is that what you 'know' about reading and writing will determine what you observe in children's literacy development. You bring to the observation what you already believe.

We need to design procedures that limit the possibilities of being in error or being misled by our observations. One way we can do this is to make certain that a wide range of measures or observations is used. Probably no one technique is reliable on its own. When important decisions are to be made we should increase the range of observations we make in order to decrease the risk that we will make errors in our interpretations.

For example, a word test should never be used in isolation because it assesses only one aspect of early reading behaviours. So does retelling. The child is learning more about letters, and about how print is written down, and how to form letters and write words, and something about letter-sound relationships, and teachers need to know how learning is proceeding in each of these areas. That is why the observation tasks described in this Survey range across each of these areas of knowledge.

It is imperative, also, that we attend to the reliability

of our observations. An unreliable test score means that if you took other measures, at around the same time or at another time, you might get very different results. We have to be concerned with whether our assessments are reliable because we do not want to alter our teaching, or decide on a child's placement, on the basis of a flawed judgement. We need to be able to rely on the data from which we make our judgements.

It is important that we use tasks that are authentic. The word authentic has arisen among educators because many tests of reading and writing and spelling are being challenged as not valid measures of real world literacy activities. One of the current criticisms of the multiple choice type of test items is that they are a special type of task not found in real life; they are a test device with no real world reference. It will be better if we can find sound assessment procedures which reflect what the learner is mastering or struggling with. (Concepts About Print was designed to have such authenticity 20 years before the word appeared in the assessment field.)

Characteristics of observation tasks

All the observation tasks which I will discuss were developed in research studies. I like to call them observation tasks but they do have the qualities of sound assessment instruments with reliabilities and validities and discrimination indices established in research studies.

These observation tasks can be justified not only by theories of measurement: other theories are taken into account, from the psychology of learning, from developmental psychology, from studies of individual differences, and from theories about social factors and the influences of contexts on learning.

The observation tasks were *not* designed to produce samples of work which go into portfolios; they were designed to make a teacher attend to how children work at learning in the classroom. It is useful to supplement our observations of children's portfolio work by systematic observation tasks, because portfolio products are often channelled by the teacher's ways of teaching or expectations, and sometimes a different kind of observation task will confront the teacher with a new kind of evidence of a child's strengths or problems.

The observation tasks in this Survey do not simplify the learning challenge. They are designed to allow children to work with the complexities of written language.

They do not measure children's general abilities, and they do not look for the outcomes of a particular programme. They tell teachers something about how the learner searches for information in printed texts and how that learner works with that information.*

---

*To help teachers attend to features of oral language one could recommend Clay et al. (1983) and Cazden (1988). A standard story retelling task (McKenzie 1989; Morrow 1989) is also helpful to sensitise teachers to individual differences in the child's growing control over constructing stories.

2 | READING AND WRITING: PROCESSING THE INFORMATION IN PRINT

Marie Clay

THE READING PROCESS

Reading, like thinking, is a complex process. The reader has to produce responses to the words the author wrote. In some way the reader has to match his thinking to the author's.

You will be familiar with the old game 'Twenty Questions' or 'Animal, Vegetable or Mineral'. Reading is something like that game. The smarter readers ask themselves the most effective questions for reducing uncertainty; the poorer readers try lots of trivial questions and waste their opportunities to reduce their uncertainty. They do not put the information-seeking processes into effective sequences.

Many instructional programmes direct their students to the trivial questions. All readers, from five-year-old beginners on their first books to the effective adult reader, need to use:

- their knowledge of how the world works
- the possible meanings of the text
- the sentence structure
- the importance of order of ideas, or words, or of letters
- the size of words or letters
- special features of sound, shape, and layout
- and special knowledge from past literary experiences,

before they resort to left to right sounding out of chunks or letter clusters or, in the last resort, single letters. Such an analysis suggests that the terms 'look and say' or 'sight words' or 'phonics' are grossly simplified explanations of what we need to know or do in order to be able to read.

Reading for meaning involves the reader in working with information from all these resources. Even after only one year of instruction, the high progress reader operates on print in an integrated way in search of meaning, and reads with high accuracy and high self-correction rates. He reads with attention focused on meaning. What he thinks the text will say can be checked by looking for sound-to-letter associations. He also has several ways of functioning according to the type of reading material (genre) or the difficulty level of the material. Where he cannot grasp the meaning with higher level strategies he can engage a lower gear and use another strategy drawing on knowledge of letter clusters or letter-sound associations, but all the while the competent reader manages to maintain a focus on the messages of the text.

On the other hand, the low progress reader or reader at risk tends to operate on a narrow range of strategies. He may rely on what he can invent from his memory for the language of the text but pay no attention at all to visual details. He may disregard obvious discrepancies between his response and the words on the page. He may be looking so hard for words he knows and guessing words from first letters that he forgets what the message is about. Unbalanced ways of operating on print can become habituated when they are practised day after day. They become very resistant to change. This can begin to happen in the first year of formal instruction.

That is why systematic observation of what the child can do and where his new learning takes him is so important in the first year of school. Close and individual attention from a teacher at this stage can help children to operate on print in more appropriate ways, so they can learn to work effectively under normal classroom conditions and make progress at average rates.

In recent years there have been shifts in our understanding of some psychological processes and yet old theories remain encapsulated in our teaching methods and assumptions. Some of these concepts need to be reviewed here.

By far the most important challenge for the teacher of reading is to change the ways in which the child operates on print to get the messages. We must look briefly at the model of the reading process that is implied here. (A more extensive discussion related to the early years of formal schooling is available in Clay 1991.)

1   Reading involves messages expressed in language. Usually it is a special kind of language which is found in books. Children bring to the reading situation a control of oral language but the oral language dialect differs in important ways from the written language dialect. Although some children may not speak the same oral dialect as the teacher almost all have a well-developed language system and they communicate well in their homes and communities. They have control of most of the sounds of the language, a large vocabulary of words which are labels for quite complex sets of meanings, and they have flexible ways of constructing sentences.

2   Reading also involves knowing about the conventions used to print language—direction rules, space formats, and punctuation signals for new sentences, new speakers, surprise or emphasis, and questions. These are things which the skilled reader does not think about because he responds giving only minimal attention to such conventions of print. But for the beginning reader they are the source of some fundamental confusions.

3   Reading involves visual patterns—clusters of words/syllables/blends/letters—depending on how one wants to break the patterns up. Processing information from the printed page is so fast in skilled readers that it is only by drastically altering the reading situation in experiments that we can show how adults scan text to pick up cues from patterns and clusters of these components. Young children tend to operate on visual patterns in very personal ways and slowly enough for us to observe some of what they do.

4   The flow of oral language does not always make the breaks between words clear and young children have some difficulty breaking messages up into words. They have even greater difficulty breaking up a word into its sequence of sounds and hearing the sounds in sequence. This is not strange. Some of us have the same problem with the note sequences in a complicated melody.

These are four different areas of learning which facilitate reading. Language was discussed first because the meanings embodied in print are of high utility, especially if one already knows something about the topic of the text. Language has two powerful bases for prediction in reading. The first is the meanings and the second is the sentence structures. A third, less reliable and sometimes confusing and distorting source of cues exists in the letter-sound relationships. Theoretical analyses tell us that it is the consistencies in the spelling patterns or clusters of letters, rather than the letter-sound relationships, that assist the mature reader's reading. If that is where the consistencies lie that is where the human brain will find and use them.

The conventions that printers use to print language also need to be learned because we need to attend to the visual information in ways that follow the rules of the printer's code, more or less.

Visual information is essential for fluent correct responding and skilled readers tend to use visual knowledge in a highly efficient way, scanning for enough detail to check on the messages of the text. The beginning reader must discover for himself how to do this scanning and how to visually analyse print to locate cues and features that distinguish between letters and words.

The sound sequences in words (which linguists call the sequence of phonemes) are also used in rapid reading to anticipate a word from a few cues or to check a word one is uncertain about. This requires two kinds of detailed analysis in strict coordination: the analysis of the sounds in sequence and the visual analysis in left to right sequence.

Most children can become literate. They can learn literacy behaviours if the conditions for learning are right for them as individual learners. Three shifts in knowledge about learning have raised our expectations for greater success for more children in literacy learning today. Firstly, it is accepted today that experience counts in cognitive functioning, and some of what we thought of as 'given' in intelligence is learned during the process of cognitive development. Secondly, there has been a shift away from the belief that 'in some rough and ready way' achievement matches to general measured intelligence. We have known for nearly 30 years that when you look at the children who are over-achieving, for example when a child is reading well and several years above his mental age level, then the supposed match between achievement and intelligence must be questioned.

If we put the last two concepts together—that some part of the cognitive process is learned or realised through experience and that achievement ages do not necessarily match mental ages—there is plenty of scope for teaching and learning experience to bring about a change in children's attainments.

The third revision of an older position is in the area of brain functioning. When psychologists wrote about the brain as similar to a telephone exchange, association theories of learning were popular and people were thought of as having better or poorer telephone exchanges, prewired to do poorer or better jobs. Without discarding the idea that people may differ in the brain structures they have to work with, it is now known that for complex functions the brain probably constructs circuits which link several quite different parts of the brain and that such circuits only become functional for those persons who learn to do those things. We create many of the necessary links in the brain as we learn to engage in literate activities. If we do not engage in literate activities we do not create those linked pathways.

THE WRITING PROCESS

The exploration of literacy that preschool children do is even more obvious in their early attempts to write. They explore the making of marks on paper, from scribble to letter-like forms, to some letter shapes, often part of their own name, to favourite letters and particular words and then they acquire more letters and more words, but all the time invented forms and invented words intrude into their productions as they explore possibilities. After entry to school children work quite hard to understand the conventions of the printer's code, the 'rules' of writing language down, mastering some of these quite early, and taking a surprisingly long time to understand the functions of others, for example, the space concept, or the importance of order, or the difference that orientation of letters makes to what they stand for.

For example, Amanda's writing looks like a jumble of disoriented letters but the teacher who observed her rated it a good attempt at the observation task which records how well the child can hear the sounds in words.

In fact preschool children can respond to and learn about visual features of print, know some letters, write some words, make up pretend writing as letters to people, or dictate stories they want written, and all this before they have begun to consider how the words they say may be coded into print, and in particular how the sounds of speech are coded in print. The biggest hurdle is to learn when this coding follows regular rules or patterns, and what are the alternate or irregular coding patterns that might be needed.

Without a feel for the conventions of print the child cannot bring what he knows about letters and words to bear on the writing task, and without some skill at hearing the sounds within words, he has no chance of learning

Amanda's writing

Line 2

START
HERE   Line 1

Line 3

Line 1: The (və) bus is coming It
Line 2: teg em tel to ereh pots lliw
Line 3: on

(Courtesy of M. Fried, Ohio State University)

letter-sound relationships. He may memorise some letter sequences of words he likes to write using visual information and a memory for the motor movements. But until he begins to notice that sounds in his speech can be written in consistent ways he has no way of attempting to write a word which he has not memorised.

So, there are many facets to the writing process just as there are to the reading process, and they can be described in much the same way. Writing involves messages expressed in language, and the writer must compose these. They flow directly from his own language competencies. Writing involves visual learning of letter features and letter forms, and patterns of letters in clusters or in words, and mingling these with what one knows about the conventions of the printer's code. Writing also involves the young writer in listening to his own speech to find out which sounds he needs to write, and then finding the letters with which to record those sounds.

As the young writer works earnestly to get his message down on paper he is, like the reader, working up and down the various levels at which we can analyse language—message, sentence, word, letter cluster, or letter-sound. As a reader he may ignore some of the information in print, leaning upon the anchor points of the information he knows. In writing. however, there is no other way to write than letter by letter, one after the other; it is an analytical activity which takes words apart. He may omit letters, or use substitutes for the ones in orthodox spelling, but he is forced by the nature of the task to act analytically on print when he is writing.

Composing orally something that he wants to write, or wants a teacher to write for him, is not easy for all children and the quality of composition, in telling stories or relaying information, improves as children immerse themselves in the task (Paley 1981).

There is, however, a tedious time when the child must work out for himself how the composition can be recorded, and what he, as the writer, has to do to get the story down on paper. Both the composition and the scribing sides of the task can be approached with success by the preschool child, or in the first year of school.

In summary, teachers aim to produce independent readers whose reading and writing improve whenever they read and write. In the independent student:

- early strategies are secure and habituated
- the child *monitors* his own reading or writing
- he *searches* for cues in word sequences, in meaning, in letter sequences
- he *discovers* new things for himself
- he *cross-checks* one source of cues with another
- he *repeats* as if to *confirm* his reading or writing
- he *self-corrects*, assuming the initiative for making cues match, or getting words right
- he *solves* new words by these means.

3 ASSISTING YOUNG CHILDREN MAKING SLOW PROGRESS

Marie Clay

TRADITIONAL APPROACHES

Since I first began to teach children to read more than 40 years ago the teaching problems have remained much the same, although the services have increased and improved and the percentage of children needing special help may have been reduced. What we do have today is an awareness of literacy learning among teachers, parents and the community that did not exist in the 1950s when we were trying to create that awareness.

With the growth of community interest there has been a proliferation of naive ideas about what reading is and what reading difficulties are. Incorrect and misleading ideas are found in the media each week. The following are two examples.

- Critics of the schools often assume that people differ in intelligence but they expect all people to reach a *similar* level in reading. These two expectations are contradictory.
- Completely erroneous statements are made about words *seen in reverse* or *the brain scrambling the signals for the eyes* or *squares looking like triangles*. There is no evidence to support such nonsensical descriptions of how our brains work as we read.

These errors of understanding arise from adults who make superficial or poor observations of their own skills or who disseminate misguided interpretations of new concepts, half-understood.

By the fourth year of school a teacher will have a range of reading ability in her classroom that spreads over five or six years. The less able children will read like children in the first or second year class and her more able children will read like young high school pupils. There is a range of reading achievement for which the class teacher must provide. It comes about in part because once a certain command of reading is attained one's reading improves every time one reads. Traditionally *a child has been considered worthy of special help only if his achievement falls more than two years below the average for his class or age group. That criterion had more to do with the reliability of our achievement test instruments than with any particular learning needs of the children.*

Teachers and the educational system should make every effort to reduce the number of children falling below their class level in reading, but public opinion must learn to ask appropriate evaluative questions. If all children at every point in the range of normal variation are increasing their skill then the school is doing its job well. All children will not be able to read in the same way or at the same level any more than they can all think alike.

Let me give an example. Livia had many differences in his preschool experiences compared with the average school entrant. He was over seven years before he was able to start reading books. In his fourth year at school he was reading well at the level of children in their third year at school. In one sense he was not a reading problem. His rate of progress *once he had begun to read* was about average. Livia needed reading material and instruction *at his level* so that he could continue to learn to read and only in that sense had he a reading problem. If given harder materials to read he would work at frustration level and could even 'go backwards' because he would no longer be practising, in smooth combination, the skills he had developed so far. In this way he could become illiterate for want of appropriate pacing of his reading material.

There is a reading level below which the child may lose his skill when he moves out into the community rather than maintain it. It falls somewhere around the average 10- to 11-year-old reading achievement level. If our reading skill is not sufficient for us to practise it every day by reading the paper or notices or instructions, then we seem to lose some of the skill in much the same way as we lose a foreign language which we no longer speak.

A first requirement of a good reading programme is that all teachers check the provisions that they make for the lowest reading groups in their classes. Is the programme really catering for the range of literacy knowledge which the children have? For learning to occur it is *very* important to ensure that the difficulty level of the reading material presents challenges from which the child can learn, and not difficulties that disorganise what he already knows. If children in a low reading group are not reading for meaning, if what they read does not sound like meaningful language, if they are stuttering over sounds or words with no basis for prediction, they should be taken back to a level of reading material where they can orchestrate all the reading processes and knowledge into a smoothly functioning, message-getting process. (They will read fairly accurately with about one error in five to 10 words.)

Each classroom needs a wide range of reading books to cater for the expected range of reading skills. All children need both easy and challenging books from which they learn different things. Just as you might find it relaxing on holiday to pick up a light novel, an Agatha Christie or a science fiction book, competent readers enjoy easy reading too. *On easy material they practise the skills they have and build up fluency.*

Perhaps one or two children in the lowest group do not seem to be able to read anything. It may be that they have been forced to read at frustration level for as long as a year or two, and they may even have *lost their initial reading skills*. Children can go backwards later in their schooling, reading worse than they did at an earlier age. Such children may need individual teaching in order to redevelop an independent attack on books.

In the lowest reading group of many classes there could be a child who has never started to learn to read. Such children may be given remedial attention two and three times a week for several years yet they do not catch up to their peers; they may gain some reading skills but do not usually make up for those years of lost learning and their associated sense of failure.

What are the ingredients of a good reading programme for children of low achievement in classroom settings? For a good programme you need a very experienced teacher who has been trained to think incisively about the reading process and who is sensitive to individual differences. You need an organisation of time and place that permits such teachers to work individually with the children who have the least skills. The teacher helps and supports the pupil in reading meaningful messages in texts which are expertly sequenced to the individual's needs.

The teacher aims to produce in the pupil a set of behaviours which will ensure a self-extending system. With a self-extending set of behaviours the more the learner reads or writes the better he gets, and the more unnecessary the teacher becomes.

The teacher expects to end up with pupils who are as widely distributed in reading as they are in the population in intelligence, mathematical achievement, sporting skills or cooking prowess. But each pupil should be making progress *from where he is to somewhere else.*

Frequently, someone approaches me with this kind of statement: 'I'm not a teacher, but I would like to help children with reading difficulties. Do you think I could?' My answer is that the best person to help a child with reading difficulties is a trained teacher who has become a master teacher of reading, and who has been trained as a specialist in reading problems. There is no room for an amateur approach to children with reading difficulties, for, unlike many human conditions, failure to read almost never ends in spontaneous recovery.

EARLY INTERVENTION

All understandings of how we read and of what the reading process is have changed in the last two decades under the impact of reports from intensive research efforts. What the older scholars recommended as techniques still have validity (for example, Fernald, 1943); the ways in which they understood the reading process do not. Theorists now look upon the reading process in a different way and that makes many of the older texts on reading out of date. It is not enough today to recommend old concepts and cures to solve reading difficulties. We now have very good reasons for discarding old concepts that lead to ineffective teaching.

If I believed for example that visual images of words had to be implanted by repetition in children's minds, and that a child had to know every set of letter-sound relationships that occur in English words before he could progress in reading then I could not explain some of my successes as a teacher. I could not explain how an 11-year-old with a reading age of eight years could make three years' progress in reading in six months, having two short lessons each week. It just would not be possible.

A good theory ought at least to be able to explain its successes.

When I surveyed research reports which measured children before remedial work, after the programmes, and then after a follow-up period, the results were almost always the same. Progress was made while the teacher taught, but little progress occurred back in the classroom once the clinical programme finished (Aman & Singh 1983). One study like this carried out in New Zealand recently had the same result. The children could not continue to progress without the remedial teacher. They were not learning reading the way that successful readers learn. *Successful readers learn a system of behaviours which continues to accumulate skills merely because it operates.* (Exceptional reading clinicians do help children to build self-extending strategies but they do not seem to do this frequently enough to influence the research findings.)

We have operated in the past on a concept of remedial tuition that worked but did not work well enough. There have been clinicians, principals, teachers, and willing folk in the community working earnestly and with commitment. Individual children have received help but the size of the problem has not been reduced. Some children were recovered, others were maintained with some improvement and some continued to fail.

Why was this so? Lack of early identification has been one reason. In other areas of special education we practise early identification. Deaf babies, our blind and cerebral-palsied preschoolers and others with special handicaps get special help to minimise the consequential aspects of their handicaps. Yet a child with reading difficulties has had to wait until the third or fourth year of school before being offered special instruction. By then the child's reading level is two years behind that of his peers. The learning difficulties of the child might be more easily overcome if he had practised error behaviour less often, if he had less to unlearn and relearn, and if he still had reasonable confidence in his own ability. Schools must change their organisation to solve these problems early. It takes a child with the most supportive teacher only three to four months at school to define himself as 'no good at that' when the timetable comes around to reading or writing activities.

Teachers and parents of 11- to 16-year-olds often believe that schools have done nothing for the reading difficulties of the young people they are concerned about. Yet the older child has probably been the focus of a whole sequence of well-intentioned efforts to help, each of which has done little for the child. This does not mean that children do not sometimes succeed with a brilliant teacher, a fantastic teacher-child relationship, a hard-working parent-child team. What it does mean is that the efforts often fail *for want of experienced teaching, and for want of persistence and continuity of efforts. They often fail because they are begun too late.*

It seemed to me that the longer we left the child failing the harder the problem became and three years was too long. The results of waiting are these.

- There is a great gap or deficit to be made up.
- There are consequential deficits in other aspects of education.
- There are consequences for the child's personality and confidence.
- An even greater problem is that the child has not only failed to learn in his three years at school, he has tried to do his work, he has practised his primitive skills and he has habituated, daily, the wrong responses. He has learned; and all that learning stands like a block wall between the remedial teacher and the responses that she is trying to get established.

A remedial programme must take what has to be unlearned into account.

Why have we tended to wait until the child was eight or more years old before offering special assistance?

- We believed, erroneously, that children mature into reading.
- We do not like to pressure children, and we gave them time to settle.
- We knew children who were 'late bloomers' (or we thought we did).
- Our tests were not reliable until our programmes were well under way and we were loath to label children wrongly or to use scarce remedial resources on children who would recover spontaneously.
- We did not understand the reading process sufficiently well.
- We thought a change of method, a search for the great solution, would one day make the reading problem disappear.
- We believed in simple, single causes such as 'not having learned his phonics'.
- Teachers have real difficulty in observing which children are having difficulty at the end of the first year of instruction, often claiming there are no such children in their schools.

In 1962 when I began my research I asked the simple question 'Can we see the reading process going wrong in the first year of instruction?' It was, in terms of our techniques at the time, an absurd question. The answer is, however, that today this can be observed by the well-trained teacher. And it is much simpler than administering batteries of psychological tests or trying to interpret the implications for reading of neurological examinations.

At the end of the first year at school, teachers can locate children who can be seen to need extra resources and extra help to unlearn unwanted behaviours or to put together isolated behaviours into a workable system. Simple observation tasks will predict well which young children who have been in instruction for one year are readers 'at risk'. The children's performance on the tasks also gives the teacher some idea of what to teach next. The second year at school can then be used as a time to catch up with the average group of children.

THE SENSITIVE OBSERVATION OF READING BEHAVIOUR

First steps in the prevention of reading difficulties can be taken in any school system by the sensitive appraisal of the individuality of school entrants, and the careful observation at frequent intervals of children's responsiveness to a good school programme. Predictive tests may be available but are prone to error because they try to estimate how well a child will perform in an activity he has not even tried yet. They can be supplemented or replaced by systematic observation and recording of what children are doing as they perform the tasks of the classroom. Observation of children's behaviour is a sound basis for the early evaluation of reading progress. Children may stray off into poor procedures at many points during the first year of instruction.

I refer here to a controlled form of observation which requires systematic, objective recording of exactly what a child does on a particular (sometimes contrived) task. It must be carried out without any accompanying teaching or teacher guidance. This contrasts with several things— observation while teaching, casual or subjective observation, or judgemental conclusions based on remembered events from fleeting observations during the teaching of many children.

Of 100 children studied in one Auckland-based study (Clay 1966, 1982) there were children making slow progress because of poor language development and whose real problem lay in their inability to form and repeat phrases and sentences. There were many children who wavered for months trying to establish a consistent direc-

tional approach to print. There were children who could not hear the separation of words within a spoken sentence, nor the sequence of sounds that occur in words. Some children attended only to the final sounds in words. Two left-handed writers had some persisting problems with direction, but so did several right-handed children. For some children with poor motor coordination the matching of words and spaces with speech was a very difficult task. But other children with fast speech and mature language could not achieve success either, because they could not slow down their speech to their hand speed. They needed help with coordinating their visual perception of print and their fast speech. There were unhappy children who were reticent about speaking or writing, and there were rebellious and baulky children. There were children of low intelligence who made slow progress with enthusiasm, and there were others with high intelligence who worked diligently and yet were seldom accurate. There were those who lost heart when promoted because they felt they were not able to cope, and others who lost heart because they were kept behind in a lower reading group.

A flexible programme which respects individuality at first, brings children gradually to the point where group instruction can be provided for those with common learning needs.

While sensitive observation during the first year of instruction is the responsibility of the class teachers, a survey of reading progress after one year of instruction should be programmed by a person responsible for organisation and evaluation of the first years in school. Such a survey is held to be desirable and practical, in addition to the observations made by class teachers.

A year at school will have given all children a chance to settle, to begin to engage with the literacy programme, to try several different approaches, to be forming good or bad habits. It is not hurrying children unduly to take stock of their style of progress a year after society introduces them to formal instruction. Indeed, special programmes must then be made available for those children who have been unable to learn from the standard teaching practices. This makes good psychological and administrative sense.

The timing of such a systematic survey will depend upon the policies of the education system regarding:

- entry to school
- promotion and/or retention.

In New Zealand continuous entry on children's fifth birthday is usually followed by fixed annual promotion to the third-year class level. This allows a flexible time allocation of 18 to 36 months for a child to complete the first two class levels according to an individual child's needs. A slow child who takes a year to settle into the strange environment of school may need extra help in the second year to make average progress before promotion to class or year three.

A different scenario would occur with fixed age of entry. Children entering school at one time (four-and-a-half to five-and-a-half, or five-and-a-half to six-and-a-half) would be surveyed within or after their first year at school. My preference would be for them to receive individual help at the beginning of the second year, having been promoted rather than retained. An alternative would be to get help to them after six months of the first year on the assumption that they could be promoted to the second-year class rather than retained. This latter procedure may lead to some unforeseen problems in that it may identify for help children who would 'take off' without help in the second six months of that first year of school.

In school systems where entry occurs at younger ages more relaxed and less urgent policies can be adopted. In systems where entry age levels tend to be higher, formal instruction tends to proceed with more urgency and waiting for a year before identifying children may not be seen as appropriate. The key point to bear in mind is that children must not be left practising inappropriate procedures for too long, but on the other hand they cannot be pressured and hurried into learning the fundamental complexities of reading and writing. This leads us back to the child who is having difficulty with school learning towards the end of his first year at school.

Each child having difficulty will have different things he can and cannot do. Each will differ from others in what is confusing, what gaps there are in knowledge, in ways of operating on print. The failing child might respond to an intervention programme especially tailored to his needs in one-to-one instruction.

THE EARLY DETECTION OF READING DIFFICULTIES

Traditionally reading difficulties have been assessed with readiness tests, intelligence tests, and tests of related skills such as language abilities or visual discrimination. These have been used to predict areas which might account for a child's reading failure. The problem with the intricate profiles that such tests produce is that while they

may sketch some strengths and weaknesses in the child's behaviour repertoire, they do not provide much guidance as to what the teacher should try to teach the child *about reading*. The child with limited language skills must still be taught to read, although some authorities advise teachers to wait until the child can speak well. The child with visual perception difficulties can be put on a programme of drawing shapes and finding paths through mazes and puzzles, but he must still be taught to read.

Many research studies have found no benefit resulting from training programmes derived directly from such test results. The pictorial and geometrical stimuli used with young retarded readers did not produce gains in reading skill. And oral language training was no more useful. This may well be because the children were learning to analyse data which they did not require in the reading task and they were not learning anything that was directly applicable in the reading activity. Again and again research points to the egocentric, rigid and inflexible viewpoint of the younger, slower or retarded reader. And yet statements on remediation just as often recommend training the child on 'simpler' materials—pictures, shapes, letters, sounds—all of which require a large amount of skill to transfer to the total situation of reading a message which is expressed in sentence form! To try to train children to read on pictures and shapes or even on puzzles, seems a devious route to reading. One would not deny that many children need a wide range of supplementary activities to compensate for barren preschool lives; but it is foolish to prepare for reading by painting with large brushes, doing jig-saw puzzles, arranging large building blocks, or writing numbers. Preparation for reading can be done more directly with written language.

Having established that printed forms are the remedial media, one can then allow that simplification, right down to the parts of the letters, may at times be required for some children. However, *the larger the chunks of printed language the child can work with, the more quickly he learns*, and the richer the network of meanings he can use. We should only dwell on detail long enough for the child to discover its existence and then encourage the use of it in isolation only when absolutely necessary. As a reader the child will use detail within and as a part of a pattern of cues or stimuli. The relationships of details to patterns in reading have often been destroyed by our methods of instruction. It is so easy for us as teachers, or for the designers of reading materials, to achieve that destruction.

There have been many attempts to match teaching

methods to the strengths of groups of children. The child with good visual perception is said to benefit from sight-word methods; the child with good auditory perception is thought to make better progress on phonic methods. One author writes: 'Children are physiologically oriented to visual or auditory learning.' Another says, 'Teaching phonics as a relatively "pure" form will place a child at a disadvantage if he is delayed in auditory perceptual ability'! Such instruction would place all children at a severe disadvantage; they would have to learn by themselves many skills that their teachers were not teaching, if they were to become successful readers.

Such matching attempts are simplistic, for English is a complex linguistic system. The way to use a child's strengths and improve his weaknesses is not to work on one or the other but to design the tasks so that he practises the weakness with the aid of his strong abilities. Rather than take sides on reading methods which deal either with sounds that are synthesised or with sentences which are analysed,

> . . . it is appropriate to select reading texts which are simple and yet retain the full power of semantic and syntactic richness, helping the child to apply his strong speaking abilities to their analysis on any level of language.

Close observation of a child's weaknesses will be needed because he will depend on the teacher to structure the task in simple steps to avoid the accumulation of confusions. For one child the structuring may be in the visual perception area. For another it may be in sentence patterns. For a third it may be in the discrimination of sound sequences. For a fourth it may be in directional learning. It is most likely to be in the bringing together of all these ways of responding as the reader works sequentially through a text.

It therefore seems appropriate to seek diagnosis of those aspects of the reading process which are weak in a particular child soon after he has entered instruction. The Observation Survey has been used to provide such information for children taught in very different programmes for beginning reading in English (in New Zealand, Scotland, Australia and the United States). Children in different programmes of instruction do not score in similar ways but the Observation Survey provides a framework within which early reading behaviour can be explored irrespective of the method of instruction. What will vary from programme to programme will be the typical scores on the tests of the Survey after a fixed time in instruction.

In what follows there is only slight emphasis on scores and quantifying progress. The real value of the Observation Survey is to uncover what a particular child controls and what operations (see below) and items he could be taught next.

Reading instruction often focuses on items of knowledge, words, letters and sounds. Most children respond to this teaching in active ways. They search for links between the items and they relate new discoveries to old knowledge. They operate on print as Piaget's children operate on problems, searching for relationships which order the complexity of print and therefore simplify it.

The end-point of *early* instruction has been reached when children have a self-extending system of literacy behaviours and learn more about reading every time they read, independent of instruction. When they read texts of appropriate difficulty for their present skills, using their knowledge of oral and written language and their knowledge of the world, they use a set of operations or strategies 'in their heads' which are just adequate for reading the more difficult bits of the text. In the process they engage in 'reading work', a deliberate effort to solve new problems with familiar information and procedures. They notice new things about words, and constructively link these things to both their knowledge of the world around them, and their knowledge of the printed language gained in their short history of successful reading of simple books. The process is progressive and accumulative. The newly noticed feature(s) of print, worked upon today, becomes the reference point for another encounter in a few days. 'Television' as a new word becomes a reference point for 'telephone' in a subsequent text. Children are working on two theories—what Smith (1978) calls their theory of the world and what will make sense, and a second theory of how written language is created. They are testing these two theories and changing them successively as they read more books.

In the Observation Survey an emphasis will be placed on the operations or strategies that are used in reading, rather than on test scores or on disabilities.

> The terms *operation* or *strategy* are used for mental activities initiated by the child to get messages from a text.

1 A child may have the necessary abilities but may not have learned how to use those abilities in reading. He will not be observed to use helpful strategies. *He must learn how to work effectively with the information in print.*

2 Or a child may have made insufficient development in one ability area (say, motor coordination) to acquire the required strategy (say, directional behaviour) without special help. *He must learn how to . . . in spite of . . .*

3 Again, a child may have items of knowledge about letters and sounds and words but be unable to relate one to the other, to employ one as a cross-check on the other, or to get to the messages in print. He is unable to use his knowledge in the service of getting to the messages. *He must learn how to check on his own learning . . . and how to orchestrate different ways of responding to complete a smooth message-getting process.*

In any of these instances the task for the reading/writing programme is to get the child to learn to use any and all of the strategies or operations that are necessary to read texts of a given level of difficulty.

There is an important assumption in this approach. Given a knowledge of some items, and a *strategy* which can be applied to similar items to extract messages, the child then has a general way of approaching new items. We do not need to teach him the total inventory of items. Using the strategies will lead the reader to the assimilation of new items of knowledge. Strategies for problem solving novel features of print are an important part of a self-extending system.

An example may help to clarify this important concept. Teachers through the years have taught children the relationship of letters and sounds. They have, traditionally, shown letters and given children opportunities to associate sounds with those letters. There seemed to be an obvious need to help the child to translate the letters in his book into the sounds of spoken words. And, in some vague way, this also helped the child in his spelling and story writing.

In our studies of children after one year of instruction we found children at risk in reading who could give the sounds of letters but who found it impossible to hear the sound sequences in the words they spoke. They could go *from letters to sounds* but they were unable to check whether they were right or not because they could not hear the sound sequence in the words they spoke. They were unable to go *from sounds to letters*. Being able to carry out the first operation, letters to sounds, probably leads easily to its inverse for many children but for some of our children at risk one strategy did not imply the other.

After six months of special tutoring Tony's progress report at the age of 6:3 (see below) emphasises not the item gains (in Letter Identification or Reading Vocabulary) but the actions or operations that he can initiate. He can analyse some initial sounds in words, uses language cues, has a good locating response, checks his predictions and has a high self-correction rate.

Tony

• (aged 5:9) has some early concepts about directionality and one-to-one correspondence but his low letter identification score and nil scores on word tests mean that he has no visual signposts with which to check his fluent book language.

• (aged 6:0) has made only slight progress in the visual area. In reading patterned text, he relies heavily on language prediction from picture clues and good memory for text, with very little use of visual information. His self-correction behaviour is almost nil, the two corrections made were on the basis of known words.

• (aged 6:3) identifies 37/54 letter symbols, has started accumulating a reading and writing vocabulary and can analyse some initial sounds in words. In reading unpatterned text, he uses language cues, a good locating response, known reading vocabulary and some initial sounds to check his predictions. He has a high self-correction rate.

An approach to literacy learning which emphasises the acquisition of reading strategies bypasses questions of reading ages and learning disabilities. It demands the recording of what the child does, on texts of specified difficulty; it refers to the strengths and weaknesses of his strategies, and compares these with a model of the strategies used by children who make satisfactory progress in reading. It assumes that the learner gradually constructs a network of strategies which make up a self-extending system, allowing the learner to continue to learn to read by reading, and learn to write by writing.

SECTION II

EARLY INTERVENTION AND SYSTEMATIC OBSERVATION FOR SPANISH SPEAKERS

4 EARLY INTERVENTION PROGRAMS IN SPANISH FOR SPANISH SPEAKERS: A RATIONALE

Kathy Escamilla
Ana María Andrade
Amelia G. M. Basurto
Olivia A. Ruiz

There are currently about 7.5 million school-aged children in the United States who enter school speaking languages other than English (Lyons 1991). About 70 percent of these students speak Spanish as a first language (Lyons 1991). The number of Spanish-speaking students entering U.S. schools has steadily increased over the past decade and these children constitute the fastest growing group in U.S. public schools (Brown 1992).

During the past twenty years, bilingual education programs have been widely implemented in the United States as a means of providing quality educational experiences to these Spanish-speaking language minority students. Politically, bilingual education has been extremely controversial. Research studies have established that bilingual education programs are pedagogically sound when fully implemented with well qualified staff and administrative support (Cummins 1989; Hakuta and Gould 1987; Ramírez, Yuen and Ramey 1991).

Bilingual education programs are implemented in many different ways, but generally they utilize a child's native language for initial literacy development while systematically integrating English as a second language. This model has demonstrated that initial success in native language literacy provides a base for subsequent success in English (Escamilla 1987; Krashen and Biber 1988; Ramírez, Yuen and Ramey 1991; Troike 1978; Willig 1985).

Clay (1993) added this support for native language instruction: "The least complicated entry into literacy learning is to begin to read and write the language that children already know and speak. What they already know about language can then be used to power their literacy learning."

The above achievements and the overall positive impact of bilingual education programs for Spanish-speaking students are well established. However, there are some Spanish-speaking students who have not achieved the desired results in native language or second language literacy. These students, like their English-speaking counterparts, have difficulty at the beginning stages of literacy acquisition, requiring special attention or "something extra" in the way of instruction to achieve the levels of literacy and biliteracy needed to be academically successful.

Typically, this something extra has taken the form of pullout compensatory programs designed to remediate the student's academic weaknesses. Pullout programs for language minority and majority students, largely funded through Title I programs in the United States, have been widely criticized during the past few years (Allington and Broikou 1988, Barrera 1989, Hornberger 1992). This criticism asserts that students continue to participate in remedial programs year after year with little evidence to suggest that their achievement improves as a result (Allington and Broikou 1988, Barrera 1989). Further, compensatory programs become "life sentences" for students: once they get in, they never get out.

An additional problem for language minority students in need of some sort of "remediation," particularly in literacy, is that the remediation is often offered in English whether or not the child has a sufficient command of it to benefit from such instruction. This approach to remediation often creates a situation in which the child may be receiving formal reading instruction in Spanish (or another native language) in the regular classroom and English reading instruction for remediation, a situation that may well result in further confusion and failure for the child (Barrera 1989).

Added to the above is the overall problem that 95 percent of the bilingual education programs for language minority students in the United States are transitional in nature. Their stated purpose is to transfer students from native language to English language programs as quickly as possible (Fradd and Tikunoff 1987). This transitional policy exacerbates difficulties for language minority students who may be struggling to learn to read in their native language. Teachers often feel pressured to get students into English reading, so they give up trying to help students become literate in their first language and simply teach in English.

The rationale for Spanish initial literacy instruction for Spanish-speaking children who are struggling to learn to read is as strong as the overall rationale for bilingual education and can be discussed around three major points. First, sound intervention programs for early elementary students who are struggling to learn to read utilize children's strengths (Clay 1989, 1991). For Spanish-speaking children, their greatest strength is their first language. Clay (1993) states that the best preparation for literacy learning is learning to talk and having many opportunities to talk. For Spanish-speaking students, learning to talk has meant learning to talk in Spanish, and it makes sense for schools to continue to encourage these children to speak and develop Spanish and to use Spanish as their springboard to literacy.

Second, there are universal literacy concepts that can be acquired in any language and transferred to literacy in a second language (Modiano 1968, Cummins 1989, Escamilla 1987, Rodríguez 1988, Thonis 1981). Three of these universal literacy concepts are that literacy is symbolic; it is communicative; and it is structured around certain discourse rules. Further, behaviors such as habits, attitudes, motivation, and self-esteem (believing in one's ability to become literate) can also most easily be developed in the native language of the children. Once developed, all of these skills, habits, and attitudes transfer easily to second language literacy situations (Ambert 1988). Early intervention programs in Spanish, therefore, can guide children in their development of these universal aspects of literacy and provide a foundation that can later be used to develop literacy in English.

Third, becoming literate requires more than knowledge of the orthographic, linguistic, and structural system of a language. Literate behavior requires an understanding of the schematic and cultural concepts of a language. *Children who do not speak English are not simply linguistically unique, they have cultural experiences and schemata that also differ from dominant-culture English-speaking students.* In a review of research related to literacy and cultural issues, Ferdman (1990) concluded that cultural schema and cultural identity mediate, to a great extent, the process of becoming literate. Further, the connections between literacy and culture must be fully acknowledged and better understood in order to achieve the goal of literacy acquisition for all.

Giroux (1985) further asserts that when a child perceives a writing task or a text and its symbolic contents as belonging to and reaffirming his or her cultural identity, it is more likely that he or she will become engaged and that individual meaning will be constructed or derived. In contrast, those tasks and symbols that deny or devalue aspects of the individual's cultural identity or even those that are neutral in relation to it may be approached differently and with less personal involvement.

Bruner (1990) states that it is culture *not* biology that shapes human life and the human mind; therefore cultural relevancy is a crucial component of an effective literacy program. In a discussion about the role of culture in becoming literate, Barrera (1992) states that teaching children to become literate involves viewing them not only as readers and writers but as meaning makers actively involved in constructing meaning during reading and writing. Meaning making is influenced by culture in several important ways.

Culture consists of the understandings of knowledge shared by members of a group of people. Much of this knowledge, is not conscious knowledge; it is largely tacit and taken for granted: "Once learned, it becomes what *one sees with*, but seldom what *one sees*" (Hutchins [1980] in Barrera [1992], p. 12). People are not born with culture, they are born into a culture, and therefore their entry into meaning is through culture.

The above notions of the relation of culture to literacy have serious instructional implications for literacy educators, the broadest of which is that one cannot validly teach reading and writing as meaning-making processes without taking into account the cultural dimensions of meaning and meaning making (Barrera 1992).

It follows, then, that it is not enough for teachers of literacy to have theories of language and learning. In order for them to engage children from a plurality of language and cultural backgrounds in the process of "meaning making," they must also have a theoretical understanding of culture and its relationship to literacy and literature. Without specific knowledge in this area, the integrity of reconstructed programs such as this one is jeopardized.

As Ferdman (1990) concludes, if a person engaged in a literacy learning situation does not have the capability to derive and create meaning in a culturally significant way, he or she will become less, not more, literate as a result.

The use of Spanish in early intervention literacy programs for Spanish-speaking students is not only important because it provides linguistic support, but also because it creates a culture-sensitive environment that enables the school to utilize the students' cultural schemata as well as their linguistic competence as support systems to create the inner control and meaning construction needed to become literate.

The plethora of literature discussed above establishes the desirability of using Spanish as the medium for developing literacy in Spanish-speaking children in U.S. schools. This literature also provided the impetus for the development of an early intervention program in Spanish to assist Spanish-speaking students who were struggling to learn to read. This early intervention program has been given the name *Descubriendo La Lectura* (Discovering Reading). As a part of the overall program development, a Spanish Observation Survey (*Instrumento de Observación de los Logros de la Lecto-escritura Inicial*) was also created. Both projects paralleled the work of Marie Clay. This development was undertaken in 1988 at a large urban school district in Tucson, Arizona.

In creating a Spanish Observation Survey, the creators quickly realized that development involved more than a mere translation. To truly create an observation instrument that reflected the language and culture of Spanish-speaking children in the United States, it was necessary to *reconstruct* the English Observation Survey. The reconstruction was then followed by field testing to establish the validity and reliability of the observational tasks that had been re-created in Spanish. Field testing also established the credibility and feasibility of systematic observation in Spanish beyond the point of theoretical supposition. A summary of the research conducted to establish the validity and reliability of the Spanish Observation Survey is included in the next chapter.

To summarize, research results related to literacy ac-

quisition provide a compelling rationale for literacy development in a child's first language. For Spanish-speaking children, then, literacy development in Spanish is strongly encouraged.

As a way of helping teachers to observe the emergence of literacy and literate behaviors in Spanish, the creators of the Spanish Observation Survey utilized the same theoretical framework that guided the development of the English Observation Survey created by Clay (1989, 1993). The Spanish Observation Survey is the tool that allows bilingual education and Spanish-speaking teachers to engage in systematic observation of children learning to read and write in Spanish.

Development of the survey in this book utilized the knowledge base and theoretical frameworks from both the fields of Bilingual Education and the work of Dr. Marie Clay for the purpose of addressing a large and growing need in the United States. This need is for ways to assist Spanish-speaking children who are having difficulty learning to read without prematurely submersing them in English and/or without permanently placing them in classes for "slow learners."

The projected growth of Spanish-speaking students in U.S. schools (35 percent over the next decade [Lyons 1991]), coupled with the continued over-representation of these students in remedial programs makes endeavors such as this one significant for policy makers and practitioners. Moreover, these efforts are imperative if the academic potential of Spanish-speaking students in our country is to be realized.

Full implementation of Spanish literacy programs in U.S. schools with bilingual education programs is one vehicle to encourage and promote the academic development of Spanish-speaking students. Efforts at full implementation can be greatly enhanced by providing bilingual education and Spanish-speaking teachers with tools such as *El Instrumento de Observación* (the Spanish Observation Survey) along with assistance in learning methods of systematic observation. It was with this goal in mind that this instrument was reconstructed from English into Spanish.

As stated before, it is important to note that the observation tasks outlined in this book were developed for use with Spanish-speaking students in the United States. The linguistic repertoire of this group of students varies greatly, ranging from students who are monolingual in Spanish and speak no English to students who are predominately Spanish speakers but speak some English to students who are fairly proficient in both languages but may have a personal preference for one language over the other.

The observation tasks presented in this book have been carefully constructed to allow the observer not only to observe child behaviors in Spanish, but to observe a child whose oral language and emergent literacy behaviors are a product of two languages (English and Spanish) that daily interact with each other.

Children who learn two languages simultaneously have carried various labels in the literature including mixed dominant, bilingual, and/or code-switchers. They have also been given more negative labels such as semi-lingual and alingual (Medina and Escamilla 1992a, 1993; Whitmore and Andrade 1989). Researchers in the field of bilingual education have long argued against the use of negative labels such as semi-lingualism for mixed dominant children (Commins and Miramontes 1989, Medina and Escamilla 1992b, Skutnabb-Kangas 1981). In spite of the arguments against such negative labels, educational programs frequently view mixed dominance, especially when manifested through code-switching behaviors in oral language, as a problem or a deficit in need of correction.

In contrast, our findings as we have developed *El Instrumento de Observación* have led us to agree with other researchers that code-switching is a natural linguistic, sociocultural phenomena when children live in environments where two languages and cultures come into contact. Consequently, code-switching is viewed as an asset not a problem.

As we developed and field-tested *El Instrumento de Observación,* we were able to go beyond oral language to observe how children use two languages to process and construct meaning from text. Our study of code-switching behaviors in emergent literacy situations is only at a beginning level at this point. However, all of the observation tasks presented and discussed in Chapters 6 and 7 include protocols and suggestions for recording childrens behaviors when they use English and Spanish concurrently in emergent literacy situations. Examples of how two languages were used concurrently by children as we developed this observation survey are also presented in Chapters 6 and 7. More important, these observation tasks give children credit for what they know, no matter which language they use to express that knowledge.

Further, more studies that observe how children use two languages when they begin to read and write are needed in order to help us better understand how children use input and cues from multiple linguistic systems to become literate.

THE RECONSTRUCTION OF THE ENGLISH OBSERVATION SURVEY INTO SPANISH: AN OVERVIEW AND DISCUSSION OF ISSUES

5

Kathy Escamilla
Ana María Andrade
Amelia G. M. Basurto
Olivia A. Ruiz

There are numerous considerations to be addressed when adapting an English language program for students from other cultural and linguistic groups. To reconstruct an observation survey such as this one, issues that needed to be considered included differences between Spanish and English in language structure, sound systems, syntax, and semantics as well as cultural differences. Further, it was crucial that the observation survey *not* be a literal translation, but that it be a conceptual reconstruction. The process of adaptation began in 1988 and was undertaken by three bilingual education teachers in Arizona who are native Spanish speakers—Chicanas—and who are sensitive to cultural and linguistic diversity. In 1989, the three original creators invited a researcher from the University of Arizona to work with them to design a research agenda to document and validate the development of *El Instrumento de Observación* (Spanish Observation Survey) and the early intervention Spanish literacy program *(Descubriendo La Lectura)*, which is a reconstruction of Reading Recovery into Spanish. The project researcher is also bilingual and has twenty-five years of experience in the field of bilingual/bicultural education.

These creators had already learned to administer the English Observation Survey and were participants in a yearlong intensive training related to English Reading Recovery. While learning the theoretical framework of the English Observation Survey, they began to construct an equivalent version in Spanish (later termed a reconstruction). Reconstruction of the English Observation Survey into Spanish took one year and was followed by two sets of research studies designed to establish the validity and reliability of the reconstructed Spanish survey (see Escamilla 1992a; Escamilla, Basurto, Andrade and Ruíz 1992).

The reconstructed Spanish survey *El Instrumento de Observación*, like the English Observation Survey, consists of six observational tasks that collectively provide a profile of a student's reading repertoire. These observational tasks include: (1) Registro Progresivo del Texto *(Running Records of Text Reading)*; (2) Identificación de Letras *(Letter Identification)*; (3) Prueba de Palabras *(Word Test)*; (4) Conceptos del Texto Impreso *(Concepts About Print)*; (5) Escritura de Vocabulario *(Writing Vocabulary)*; and (6) Oír y Registrar Sonidos en Palabras— Prueba de Dictado *(Hearing and Recording Sounds in Words—Dictation)*. Each of these observation tasks, along with administration and scoring directions and criteria, will be discussed, in detail, in the following chapters. This chapter provides a discussion of the issues and complications that arise as materials and procedures, originally developed for one group of students, are subsequently reconstructed for a different ethnolinguistic group.

When materials originally created for one linguistic group are translated into another language, serious threats to validity and reliability are posed. After the Spanish Observation Survey *(El Instrumento de Observación)* was developed, it was determined that there was a need to conduct research studies to establish the validity and reliability of this newly created survey. These studies were conducted at two different times and with two different groups of students. The first study took place during school year 1989–90 with one hundred ninety students from southern Arizona (see Escamilla, Basurto, Andrade and Ruíz 1992), and again in 1991–92 with three hundred Spanish-speaking first-grade students from the states of Arizona, Texas, and Illinois (see Escamilla 1992a).

Validity studies of *El Instrumento de Observación* conducted in 1991–92 examined concurrent, construct, and content validity. Concurrent validity was established by comparing the six observation tasks on *El Instrumento de Observación* to the Aprenda norm-referenced Spanish Reading Achievement Test. Construct validity was established by comparing each of the six observation tasks on *El Instrumento de Observación* to each other in order to determine the extent of correlation between observation tasks. Content validity was examined through a back translation of the Spanish survey. The back translation involved having the materials that had been developed in Spanish translated back into English by persons who were not familiar with the original English version and then comparing the English obtained from the back translation to the original English.

Results of the tests of concurrent validity are reported in Chapter 7 for each observation task. Construct validity correlation coefficients ranged from .52 to .83 indicating that each observation task had a strong and positive correlation to other tasks in the survey. Results of the tests of content validity via the back translations will be discussed in greater detail below, and issues related to these results are probably the most interesting to persons who may be interested in developing the observation survey in other languages.

Because of the varied population of Spanish speakers in the United States and the world and the wide variety of dialects of Spanish spoken, it was crucial to apply an additional test of validity. This validity check was applied to assess the degree to which *El Instrumento de Observación*, developed for Spanish-speaking Mexican-Americans in Tucson, Arizona, could be used with Spanish speakers from other cultural groups. To address the need to establish validity across dialects of Spanish, Brena and García (1993) administered *El Instrumento de Observación* to speakers of Spanish from three different dialects of Spanish. Their study included sixty first grade students in three different areas of the country (twenty in San Antonio, Texas; twenty in Chicago, Illinois; and twenty in Miami, Florida). Students in San Antonio were all Mexican American; students in Chicago were all Puerto Rican, and students in Miami were all Cuban-American.

The purpose of this study was to examine whether language variation across cultural groups created significant barriers in understanding and comprehension for students taking *El Instrumento de Observación*. Students in the study took all of the observation tasks except for text reading *(análisis actual del texto)*. Results of this study showed very little difference in either the range of scores or the mean and median scores of each of the tasks across language dialects. Further, for all three language groups, the range, mean, and median scores were very close to those of students in Tucson. As a further check of comprehension Brena and García made anecdotal observation notes as students engaged in each observation task to document areas of confusion and/or frustration. As expected there were vocabulary words that differed across dialects, and these differences manifested themselves when students engaged in the writing vocabulary task and the letter identification task were asked to identify words that began with certain letters. However, the protocols for administration of each of the observation tasks were not problematic for any of the students in the study.

Results of this study led these two researchers to conclude that *El Instrumento de Observación* is valid for use with Spanish speakers who speak a variety of dialects of Spanish and who come from divergent cultural groups.

Reliability of the Spanish survey was established using the Cronbach's Alpha method of analysis for the following observation tasks: (1) Identificación de Letras *(Letter Identification)*; (2) Prueba de Palabras *(Word Test)*; (3) Conceptos del Texto Impreso *(Concepts About Print)*; and (4) Oír y Registrar Sonidos en Palabras—Prueba de Dictado *(Hearing and Recording Sounds in Words—Dictation)*. A test/retest method of analysis was used for Escritura de Vocabulario *(Writing Vocabulary)*. The first observation task (Análisis Actual del Texto) involves reading of whole texts and conducting running records (see Chapter 6). Since there is not a finite number of items, it was not possible to conduct a reliability analysis. Nor, it should be noted, was such an analysis conducted on the English version. Reliability results for other Spanish observation tasks are reported in Chapter 7, along with a detailed discussion of administration and scoring of each observation task.

As stated above, a final measure of construct validity involved a back translation of *El Instrumento de Observación* from Spanish back into English. This was done to ascertain whether or not the content of the Spanish version was equivalent to the original English. Two back translations were completed by native Spanish speakers who were familiar with the area of literacy and thus knew professional terminology, and so on. Neither was familiar with the English Observation Survey and thus were not content biased. The completed back translations were analyzed by Dr. Marie Clay, the creator of the English Observation Survey, and by the creators of the Spanish *El Instrumento de Observación*.

Results of these analyses established that the Spanish version was more than an equivalent of the English version. It represented a major reconstruction of the conceptual framework of the English observation tasks from English to Spanish. The discussion below is meant to outline reconstruction issues that were considered for each observation task as it was reconstructed from English to Spanish.

OBSERVATION TASK #1—REGISTRO PROGRESIVO Y SISTEMÁTICO DE LA LECTURA DEL TEXTO (*RUNNING RECORDS OF TEXT READING*)

This observation task involves the reading of whole texts and the taking of running records related to text reading. The task and procedures for administration are described in detail in Chapter 6. The major reconstruction issue involved in the creation of this task in Spanish was the identification and leveling of Spanish language books to be included in the observation task.

As a part of the overall development of an early identification/intervention program for Spanish-speaking students, the creators of *El Instrumento de Observación* have identified books in Spanish that can be used for both assessment and intervention. To date, more than six hundred books in Spanish have been identified. These books represent a gradient of difficulty in terms of characteristics of text and level of sophistication required for successful reading. When the reconstruction process began there were few childrens books available in Spanish. Therefore, the creators had to translate/adapt appropriate texts from English to Spanish. At that time, they quickly

realized that translated texts can be problematic because of issues related to linguistic and cultural differences.

Major considerations for reconstruction of this task into other languages must include the availability of children's books written at varying levels of difficulty in languages other than English. Or, if books are going to be adapted from English to other languages, cultural authenticity and relevance become issues and must be considered. Translations that are purely literal in their nature may create cultural confusions and/or conflicts, or they may be culturally irrelevant. As discussed throughout this book, becoming literate involves interacting with text in a meaningful way. Text interaction and meaning making are enhanced when the cultural schemata of the reader is compatible with the cultural content of the text. Conversely, in the absence of cultural congruity, text interaction may be negatively impacted.

As an example to illustrate the above, we use the book *Nuestra Abuelita* (written originally in English and titled *Our Granny* [Cowley 1986]). This story was translated into Spanish in 1986. The original story and illustrations depict a modern-day grandmother who wears jogging suits and tennis shoes, has purple hair, and does funny things (e.g., she slides down a slide at a playground and shows her underwear, sings very loudly and off-key, and roller skates in the park). English-speaking children often find the story entertaining and see nothing offensive or unusual about the grandmother's behavior. Culturally, the grandmother in this story represents a "with it" grandmother—a desirable cultural attribute in the English-speaking world.

When this book was translated, words were changed but the illustrations were not. Consequently, the "image" of the grandmother in the book *Nuestra Abuelita* is not one that is culturally compatible with the image of a grandmother in many traditional Spanish-speaking cultures. In these cultures grandmothers do not do "crazy" things or have purple teased hair and green eye shadow. In Arizona, many Spanish-speaking children reading this book did not find the grandmother's antics entertaining. Instead, they were often embarrassed by her behavior and were glad that she was not their grandmother. This cultural incongruity created a type of confusion for them, and they had difficulty interacting with the text, enjoying the story, or wanting to reread it.

The above example is offered not to be overly critical of the story *Nuestra Abuelita*, but rather to illustrate the potential for cultural conflict and confusion when texts are adapted from one language into another.

As a part of the reconstruction process then, it is

necessary to identify and secure many children's books written in the desired language of observation and to ensure that adapted books are authentic culturally and linguistically.

As a caveat to this section, it is important to note that cultural and linguistic authenticity is a relative term. No attempt is made here to identify cultural and linguistic authenticity in a universal way for all Spanish- or English-speaking cultures. Instead, it will be incumbent upon teachers utilizing this survey to define the terms cultural and linguistic authenticity for their own region, cultural/linguistic population, and community.

OBSERVATION TASK #2— IDENTIFICACIÓN DE LETRAS (LETTER IDENTIFICATION)

This task requires students to identify letters using sounds, letter names, and/or words that start with the letter. This task is described in detail in Chapter 7. To reconstruct this task from English to Spanish, it was necessary, of course, to add the letters that exist in Spanish but do not exist in English. These include, ch, ll, ñ, and rr. The simple addition of the Spanish letters could not complete the reconstruction process for several reasons. First, the letter rr never occurs at the beginning of a word, and therefore it is not possible to observe whether children know this letter by asking them to name a word that starts with rr. Similarly, ñ occurs most often in the middle of a word, rarely at the beginning. Therefore, for these two letters, it was necessary to adjust the instructions for administration to ask children if they could name words that have their sounds (¿Sabes una palabra que tiene ese sonido?). In other words, the standard directions had to be reconstructed from English to Spanish to accommodate the conventions of the Spanish alphabet.

Since this instrument was constructed with Spanish-speaking children in the United States, it was being constructed for use with children who come into daily contact with both English and Spanish. As a result of this phenomenon, children sometimes will know some letter names and sounds in Spanish and others in English. For example, children might look at the letter Q and say— "Como Q-tips" (like Q-tips). Since this observation survey is designed to observe and utilize what a student knows, it was necessary to modify the scoring sheet in

order to give students credit for letter sounds or names they may know in English. The reconstruction of this task, then, considered letters, sounds, names, etc., that children may know in either English or Spanish.

Finally, the letter w was included in this task even though it does not exist in Spanish. Because of its occurrence in English, and the contact between English and Spanish in the United States, the creators found that many children know this letter as a result of exposure to two languages. The creators did not want to limit the opportunities for children to demonstrate what they know.

As a side note, this particular aspect of the reconstruction raised the issue of the need to expand the English Observation Survey to include letter names and sounds that other children may know in other languages and use when participating in the English Observation Survey.

OBSERVATION TASK #3—PRUEBA DE PALABRAS (WORD TEST)

Standardized word tests are based on the principle of sampling from the child's reading vocabulary. In the development of the English Observation Survey, these word lists were constructed from the most frequently occurring words in basic reading texts used in particular school systems. In New Zealand, this task was constructed from the forty-five most frequently occurring words in the twelve little books of the "Ready to Read" series. In the United States, the Scott, Foresman Basal Reading Series and the Dolch Word List were used to create this task (Clay 1993).

It would have been inappropriate simply to translate the words on either the New Zealand list or the Ohio list from English to Spanish. The fact that they represented words that frequently occurred in English reading materials did not necessarily mean they were words that were also frequently occurring in Spanish reading materials. Therefore, the reconstruction of this task into Spanish required examining Spanish reading materials and deriving lists of frequently occurring words. To accomplish this aspect of the reconstruction, three different sets of materials were examined. These included the Cornejo Spanish Word Frequency List (1980), the Santillana Spanish Basal Reading Series (1984), and the Brigance Spanish Sight Word Vocabulary List (1984).

From these materials, sixty frequently occurring words in Spanish were identified. These words were then separated into three lists. As a part of the validity and reliability studies, children were asked to read these sixty words. P-value tests were then calculated to determine the difficulty of each word. A P value is a statistical measure designed to ascertain which items on a given test or measure are the most and least difficult. On the Prueba de Palabras, P values were calculated to determine which of the 60 words were most difficult (that is, which words were most likely to be missed by children as they read them), and which were least difficult (those that were most likely to be read correctly by children). P-value results were then used to construct and order the final three lists of words in the Prueba de Palabras (*Word Test*).

The Prueba de Palabras is administered the same way in Spanish as in English and specific directions for administration and scoring are provided in Chapter 7.

OBSERVATION TASK #4— CONCEPTOS DEL TEXTO IMPRESO (*CONCEPTS ABOUT PRINT*)

The Conceptos del Texto Impreso (*Concepts About Print*) task is meant to observe what children have learned about the way we print languages. With regard to Spanish and English, there are many similarities: the layout of books such as the front and back, directionality (both languages are read in a left to right sequence with the left pages also being the first to be read), and the use of a roman alphabet with similar capital and lower case letters. In both langauges, spaces are there for a reason, punctuation marks have meaning, and the print tells the meaning. All of these concepts exist in print in both English and Spanish, and these similarities facilitated the construction of this task in Spanish.

Even with the great number of similarities, however, this task had to be reconstructed in two ways. The first was the reconstruction of the booklet required in order to conduct this observation and the second was the reconstruction of the observation guide for teachers to use as they administer this task. A detailed explanation of the administration and scoring procedures for this task is included in Chapter 7 of the book. A discussion of reconstruction issues is included below.

The English books *Stones* (Clay 1979) and *Sand* (Clay 1972) were reconstructed for this task and are titled *Las piedras* and *Arena* in Spanish respectively. Again, it was not possible to simply translate these books; they had to

be reconstructed as conceptual equivalents. Areas where conceptual equivalents were created are discussed in the following paragraphs.

First, with regard to the use of punctuation as meaning, it was necessary to add the appropriate Spanish langauge punctuation marks, including the inverted question mark and the *guión*, which is one way that direct quotations are noted in Spanish (Items 15 and 18 on both the Spanish and English versions).

Second, Item 21 observes whether or not children can identify words that are commonly reversed. In the English booklet, *Stones*, the reversible words are was/saw. Literally translated, these words become *fue/vio* (was/saw). In Spanish, they are not visually similar, nor are they words that Spanish-speaking children commonly reverse when they are reading. The challenge was to create an equivalent that would provide an opportunity to observe whether children could identify commonly reversed words in Spanish without losing the meaning of the story, *Las piedras*. The Spanish reconstruction created a sentence that maintained the meaning of the story and used the words *la/al* and *ya/ay* in *Las piedras* and *ya/ay* and *las/sal* in *Arena*. These are words that are, in fact, commonly reversed by Spanish-speaking children and could be included in the observation task without losing meaning in the story.

In the scoring sheet, Items 12–14 observe what children know about word order and letter order. The first Spanish re-creation phrased the observation task in the following way: "Un cambio del orden de las palabras" (a/one change in word order) and "un cambio del orden de las letras" (a/one change in letter order) respectively. This item is in many ways the most interesting, as little can be done about it.

In the back translations one translator translated the word *un* to be *a* and another translated the word *un* to be *one*. Both are correct as in Spanish, the word *un* can be either an indefinite article or a number.

The original English version used the word *one* and not *a*, and it was felt the maintenance of the word *one* was important so as not to confuse interpretation of the item. This presented an interesting problem because, in Spanish, there is not a more specific way to state this directive. The original Spanish re-creation was, therefore, left intact, but the number *1* will be included in parentheses after the word *un* for clarification. This entire issue illustrated the difficulty of creating translations that are completely equivalent and will present special challenges for those persons wanting to reconstruct these tasks into languages that are less similar to each other than Spanish and English.

Finally, in Spanish, unlike English, an accent mark is a significant concept about print. Accents are not mere punctuation marks because they change the meaning of words (e.g., *papa* means potato, but *papá* means father; *si* means if, but *sí* means yes). Awareness of how accents work provides the child with one more strategy to use in problem solving of texts, particularly as text reading becomes more difficult. Therefore, in the Spanish version of this task, an additional item was added (Item 19). This item allows for teachers to observe student knowledge of accent marks. For this reason, Conceptos del Texto Impreso in Spanish has twenty-five items while the English version has only twenty-four.

OBSERVATION TASK #5—ESCRITURA DE VOCABULARIO *(WRITING VOCABULARY)*

The writing vocabulary task in the English Observation Survey asks children to think of all the words they know and to write them down. They are given ten minutes for this task and may be given prompts by teachers (e.g., Can you write your name? Do you know how to write *is* or *to*?). Specific directions for administering and scoring this task are included in Chapter 7. With regard to reconstruction, this task was probably the one that most lent itself to reconstruction. Directions for administration were created in Spanish, and prompts that were used were selected from words frequently found in children's Spanish literature books.

Issues created in this task related to the scoring of the task and to the use of accent marks and tildes that exist in Spanish but not in English. Spanish uses accent marks and tildes as part of the graphemic system of the language, and this linguistic feature needed to be included in the creation of this observation task. As with Task 2 (Identificación de Letras—*Letter Identification*), Spanish-speaking children living in the United States often know how to write English words as well as Spanish words, especially words from the environmental print outside of school. Therefore, in addition to writing words like *mamá*, *libro*, *mi*, etc., many children also write words like *love*, *stop*, and *K-Mart*. Further, children who use two languages also interpret messages using two languages, and this interpretation often involves code-switching. For example, children engaged in this task

may say, "Yo sé escribir mamá" (I can write mom) and then write "mom" in English, or "Yo sé escribir te quiero" (I can write I love you) and then write "I love you" in English. Or a teacher may prompt, "¿Puedes escribir rojo?" (Can you write red?), and the child writes "red" in English, or "¿Puedes escribir papá?" (Can you write dad?), and the child writes "dad" in English.

In Spanish, unlike English, written accent marks and tildes are meaning makers. As cited earlier, the word *papa* without the accent means potato, but the same word *papá* written with an accent means dad. Therefore, the use of accent marks in Spanish is important in the observation of children's writing and is included as a part of the scoring system on this task.

Again, the purpose of doing observations is to note children's strengths. Therefore, it was decided that Spanish-speaking children who include English words on this observation task should be given credit for them. Similarly, it was decided that children who take the English Observation Survey and write words in other languages should also be given credit for this knowledge provided the teacher can read them and the words are correctly written.

OBSERVATION TASK #6—OÍR Y REGISTRAR SONIDOS EN PALABRAS— PRUEBA DE DICTADO *(HEARING AND RECORDING SOUNDS IN WORDS— DICTATION TASK)*

This observation task is called dictation because the teacher asks the child to record a dictated sentence. This dictated sentence is scored by counting the child's representation of the sounds (phonemes) by letters (graphemes). This observation task enables teachers to observe the awareness that children possess with regard to phoneme/grapheme relationships. As with other observation tasks discussed in this chapter, the directions for administration and scoring are included in Chapter 7.

Also, as with all other tasks, it was necessary to create a dictado (*dictation*) that was a conceptual equivalent rather than a literal translation. The English Observation Survey contains five different dictation sentences, each having thirty-seven sounds. In the English version, there are words that contain two letters but only one phoneme (e.g., in the word *school*, the letters *oo* represent only one sound and in the word *she*, the letters *sh* represent only one sound). The English version also includes words that have letters that do not have sounds (e.g., in the word *home*, the letter *e* does not have a sound and in the word *today*, the letter *y* does not have a sound).

In the process of reconstructing this task into Spanish, the developers created sentences that included an equivalent number of phonemic sounds, while also considering the phoneme/grapheme relationships that best represent the Spanish language. The Spanish version has four sentences, and the English version has five. This reconstruction included words that, as in English, had more than one letter with only one phonemic sound (e.g., the letters *qu* have one phonemic sound that is the same as the letter *k* in English). The letters *ll*, *rr*, and *ch* also have one phonemic sound in Spanish but are considered one letter. However, unlike English, Spanish has no silent letters that occur at the end of words. Using silent letters on a task such as this is relevant in English but not in Spanish. Therefore, no silent letters at the end of words were included in Spanish. Further, Spanish, unlike English, has several letters that phonemically have the same sound, and in order to create an authentic dictation task in Spanish, it was necessary to include these letter sounds. As an example, *ll* and *y*; *c*, *s*, and *z*; and *b* and *v* are Spanish letters that all have the same phonemic sounds, and all are letters that frequently occur in Spanish words.

The dictation sentences in the Spanish survey, then, were not translated from the English, but were DEVELOPED to create a dictation task that enables a teacher to observe a Spanish-speaking child's knowledge of the sound/symbol (phoneme/grapheme) relationship in the language. In order to give the reader a point of comparison, sentences from the Spanish and English tasks are presented below. As a final note, the Spanish sentences each contain thirty-nine phonemic sounds rather than thirty-seven as in English. Spanish words, in general, have more phonemic sounds than English words, thus necessitating the extra phonemes to create equivalent sentences.

Dictation Sentences from English Observation Survey:
I have a big dog at home. Today I am going to take him to school.
Mum has gone up to the shop. She will get milk and bread.
I can see the red boat that we are going to have a ride in.
The bus is coming. It will stop here to let me get on.
The boy is riding his bike. He can go very fast on it.

Oraciones del Dictado en Español (Spanish Dictation Sentences with English Translations):
Tengo un perro en la casa. Lo llevo al parque conmigo.
(I have a dog at home. I take him to the park with me.)
Papá está en casa. Dice que vamos a jugar a la pelota.
(Dad is at home. He says we are going to play ball.)
Yo tengo una gata café. Le gusta dormir en mi cama.
(I have a brown cat. She likes to sleep in my bed.)
Ya viene el tren. Se va a parar aquí. Nos vamos a subir.
(Here comes the train. It is going to stop here. We're going to get on.)

As noted at the beginning of this chapter, there are numerous issues that need to be considered when adapting materials developed for one language group into another language. The developers of the Spanish survey, *El Instrumento de Observación*, deliberated these issues at length as they created the tasks included in this book. As a result, the tasks presented in the following chapters represent tasks that are conceptually equivalent to those in the English Observation Survey. At the same time, these tasks were constructed in a manner that utilized the structural and semantic system of the Spanish language as a second point of departure to ensure authenticity in development.

SECTION III

THE SPANISH OBSERVATION SURVEY, PARTS ONE AND TWO

6 TOMANDO REGISTROS PROGRESIVOS Y SISTEMÁTICOS DE LA LECTURA DEL TEXTO

(Taking Running Records of Reading Texts)

Kathy Escamilla
Ana María Andrade
Amelia G. M. Basurto
Olivia A. Ruiz
with Marie Clay

The Observation Survey that Clay developed and that has subsequently been reconstructed in Spanish has been recommended for use as the need arises with children during their first year of school. It is one way of escaping from the problems of readiness tests. The observation tasks discussed in this chapter and the next can be used to supplement the observations that teachers make as they work alongside children. These include:

- registro progresivo *(running records)*
- identificación de letras *(letter identification)*
- conceptos del texto impreso *(concepts about print)*
- prueba de palabras *(word test)*
- escritura *(writing)*
- oír y registrar sonidos en palabras—dictado *(hearing and recording sounds in words—dictation).*

The observation tasks provide for a standard or repeatable way of comparing a child's performance over a period of time. The tasks enable teachers to observe children at work, noting all their responses (successful and unsuccessful). Teachers can then summarize where children are in their understanding of written language and can use this as the foundation for what those children are ready to learn next. *In complex learning, what is already known provides the learner with a useful context within which to embed new learning.*

At some point, not later than the end of the first year at school, it is a good idea to get a profile of learners on all these observation tasks because they cover areas of learning that underpin successful progress in reading and writing. If time does not permit individual testing of a whole class, then the teacher should decide which children s/he knows are reading and writing well and use the whole set of observation tasks with the lower half of his/her class. This will give him/her more information than giving only half the measures to all pupils in his/her class.

A set of standard observation procedures for recording reading and writing behaviors has a number of classroom applications. Various kinds of bias can affect such observations, and it is necessary to make our interpretations as reliable as we can. This can be achieved by:

- using standard procedures
- becoming skilled at applying the procedures
- using a wide range of observations that can be checked one against the other.

The procedures described in Chapters 6 and 7 have been found useful for monitoring the progress of beginning readers and writers and for detecting reading difficulties early. In the light of recent theoretical discussions of literacy learning it is desirable:

- to observe precisely what children are saying and doing
- to use tasks that are close to the learning tasks of the classroom (rather than standardized tests of reading or spelling)
- to observe what children have been able to learn (not what they have *not* been able to learn)
- to discover what reading behaviors they should now be taught from an analysis of performance as they

read, not from pictorial or puzzle material or from normative scores

• to shift the child's reading behavior from less adequate to more adequate responding by training on reading tasks (on-task activities) rather than training "skills" like visual perception or auditory discrimination (off-task activities) in the hope that such training might facilitate learning to read and write.

In this observation survey, as in the English Observation Survey, several different types of observation tasks are described. *No one task is satisfactory on its own.* Teachers are advised to apply as many as possible to the children for whom important instructional decisions must be made. Reducing the scope of our observations increases the risk that we will make erroneous interpretations. For example, the Conceptos del Texto Impreso (*Concepts About Print*) test should not be used in isolation because it assesses only one aspect of early reading behaviors. In research studies with the English version, it has been found to be an excellent predictor of subsequent reading progress, but it tells the teacher nothing about the child's knowledge of letters, or words, or letter-sound relationships. In a profile of scores a child may be high on concepts about print and low on letters and word knowledge, or vice versa. In the early stages of literacy learning, no single measure is going to inform the teacher. The child's learning is progressing on several fronts at the same time, and the teacher must know about the spurts and lags in different knowledge areas in order to make the most of his/her teaching interactions with a particular child.

Without an observation of the child's attempts at text reading or writing the teacher has no idea of how the child is managing to bring some of this rather isolated knowledge to bear on more holistic literacy tasks. So text reading and text writing become of focal interest to the teacher.

To learn something about these procedures, it would be a good idea for the teacher to make three case studies. Selecting children who are in the first year of formal instruction and who are making some progress but are clearly finding the task challenging, the teacher should try out the procedures on these children, score and analyze the results, and summarize what s/he has observed. If children with a lot of literacy knowledge are the case studies, the teacher is left with less to learn from the exercise. On the other hand, the teacher needs to become familiar with the tasks before giving them to a child with little literacy knowledge. S/he is therefore advised to practice on an average child in the first year of formal instruction.

Although these tasks can be used productively to observe older readers who are struggling, it is important to first gain skill in administration and interpretation of the observation survey on the young children for whom it was designed.

WHICH CHILDREN NEED THESE DETAILED OBSERVATIONS?

After taking into account the opportunities a particular child has had to learn about literacy before s/he came to school and the time a child has been at school, the teacher should select for further study those about whom s/he needs more information, especially those who are not making good progress. This selection is made one child at a time and should occur before the end of the child's first year of instruction. In New Zealand schools this occurs on or around the child's sixth birthday (6:0), after the child has been at school one year. The survey will probably include 30 to 50 percent of the class. The time it requires is an investment in successful progress in literacy learning because more effective teaching can come from it. School principals must become convinced of this preventive need so that they accept the importance of giving time to this kind of assessment.

There are several reasons why the sixth birthday seems a better checkpoint than the end of the school year in New Zealand schools. It staggers the testing load throughout the year and therefore ensures more individual consideration for each child. At any one time in the year a complete survey of all children would be time-consuming, and the range of tests applied would tend to be reduced. Children can be selected for observation surveys according to the level of puzzlement of their teacher. When s/he is puzzled by the child's responses a teacher needs more information; if the child is learning rapidly and progressing well, s/he apparently has the information s/he needs to be an effective teacher for that child.

In addition to these intermittent observations by teachers, a school may well decide as a matter of policy to have a systematic check of those children falling in the lower half of the class at the end of the first year of instruction.

A school with a large number of children in this age-group could use *El Instrumento de Observación* with a random sample of its children to watch how learning from the beginning of one year changes the performance of the pupils by, say, the end of the school year. Notice that for this purpose only a *sample* of pupils need be tested, and in this case the purpose is not to guide the learning of individual pupils.

The Spanish survey can serve the same functions as the English Observation Survey. These include:

- To guide the learning of individual students; and
- To watch how learning from the beginning of one year changes the performance of the pupils by the end of the school year.

Further, the survey's procedures for selecting students for assessment are also recommended, particularly for those students in the lower 50 percent of a class.

It is important to note here that acquisition of literacy in Spanish is often undervalued in schools in the United States (Escamilla 1992b, 1994; Shannon 1995). Therefore, *El Instrumento de Observación* is important for other reasons as well. These include the following:

- Aside from standardized tests of reading achievement, there is a dearth of assessment materials developed in Spanish to observe emergent literacy behaviors of Spanish-speaking children.
- As a result of the dearth of assessment materials, teachers often do not know how to improve their teaching of students who are learning to read and write in Spanish. Further, principals and other teachers often conclude that if students are struggling to learn to read in Spanish, the teacher should simply "switch" to English rather than revise and revisit what the child is doing in Spanish.
- Assessment of student progress in Spanish/English bilingual education classrooms in the United States is often limited to assessment of the acquisition of oral language in English as a Second Language. This narrow view of bilingual classroom instruction and child progress prevents teachers and administrators from understanding the whole child who is developing both in literacy in his/her native language and in knowledge of two language systems.

It is hoped that *El Instrumento de Observación*, used alongside the English Observation Survey in bilingual education classrooms in the United States, will not only enable teachers to guide individual student learning and to note group learning in Spanish, but will also improve the status of Spanish in these classrooms and the larger school environment by providing equitable ways to observe and guide literacy learning of Spanish-speaking students.

WHAT TO CAPTURE IN YOUR RECORDS

The observations of literacy behaviors described in this book are controlled and not casual. Perfect performance is easy to record and that is what traditional assessment has been concerned with. When the performance is less than perfect there are opportunities to record the work done by the child as s/he tries to puzzle it out. This reveals something of the processes by which the child monitors and corrects his/her own performance. When s/he encounters something new we can observe how s/he approaches the novel thing and what s/he learns from the encounter.

For example, one thing that readers do as they read is correct some of the errors without any prompting. Observing this we must ask How can this be? Why does the child do that? One might reply that it's something in his/her memory. But when one asks what cues the child might have been using, consistencies are found. The child gathers up cues from the structure of the sentence, or the meaning of the message, or the visual cues of the letters or letter order. We can infer from the kinds of errors and self-corrections that children make, together with their comments, much of what they are attending to. The learning work that goes on at these moments of choosing between possible responses is captured in a running record of reading or the child's independent effort to write a story.

As the child learns to talk in the preschool years s/he produces many ungrammatical sentences and uses words in unusual ways. Researchers have recorded that the errors of the two-year-old disappear as s/he gains more control over language, but they report new kinds of errors in the three-year-old who is trying new things. This can be seen in early literacy learning too. Partially correct responses do not disappear because the child is always trying new things; gaining control over some simple responses frees the child to make partially correct attempts in some new area of learning. And this continues throughout his/her schooling and into adulthood.

So the observation records should contain all the

behaviors the child produces on the task, including the comments s/he makes about what s/he is doing!

OBSERVING TEXT-READING BEHAVIOR WITH RUNNING RECORDS

Stories to assess text reading would best be selected from readily available reading materials used within the regular classroom program.

Text difficulty and text type

No matter what language a child first learns to read, there are some universal expectations of developing reading behaviors. These are outlined in the next few paragraphs. Throughout schooling, reading progress is indicated by satisfactory reading of increasingly difficult texts. New strategies are developed by the reader to cope with increases in the difficulty level of the text when complexities like multisyllabic words or literary forms of sentence structure or new kinds of texts (genres) are introduced.

When the text is close to the natural language of the young child the frequently occurring words of languages such as Spanish and English are read over and over again, and the combinations of sounds typically found in words in these languages and used by young children occur in their natural frequencies. These frequencies are the naturally occurring equivalents of vocabulary and letter-sound controls imposed by basal series authors in the past on many texts for young readers. Their existence in all texts seems to have been overlooked by the advocates of texts with controlled vocabulary.

If the young child is moving up through texts of increasing levels of difficulty that use childlike language and exercise a minimum of control over structures and vocabulary, and if s/he achieves 90 to 95 percent accuracy by the end of a normal teaching contact with that material, then s/he will be getting the opportunity to practice both the words s/he needs to learn and the clusters of sounds in those words that will help him/her to analyze new words.

The "ifs" in the last paragraph imply that we must get reliable measures of how well children read their books because this is important information for planning day-to-day instruction. Running records, described below, have proved useful in this respect both in Spanish and English.

The pivotal observation among all these observation tasks, without which all others could be misleading, is a running record of text reading *(registro progresivo)*. Accounts of how teachers use these in their classroom activities are found in *Reading in the Junior Classes* (Department of Education 1985). The running record is similar to Goodman and Burke's miscue analysis (1972), but it is particularly useful for the teacher in his/her day-to-day activities of the classroom, especially if s/he teaches young children. Running records are taken without marking a prepared script. They may be done on any piece of paper. With practice, teachers can take a running record at any time, anywhere, on any text because the behavior of the moment needs to be captured and because the opportunity arises. Teachers do not need a tape recorder. They do not have to carry out a long subsequent analysis of the record, and they do not need a technical knowledge of linguistic concepts to derive benefit from the record.

Classroom teachers can use running records for instructional purposes (see Department of Education 1985) to guide them in their decisions about any of the following:

- evaluating text difficulty
- grouping and regrouping of children
- accelerating a child
- monitoring progress of children
- allowing different children to move through different books at different speeds while keeping track of (and records of) individual progress
- observing particular difficulties in particular children.

For critical decisions such as those made in a survey to find the children having most difficulty, to provide special and supplementary assistance, to make decisions about promotion, or to inform a psychologist of the child's progress, it would be wise to obtain running records on materials from at least three levels of difficulty:

- an easy text (95 to 100 percent correct)
- an instructional text (90 to 94 percent correct)
- a hard text (80 to 89 percent correct).

In practice, teachers in New Zealand have assumed that an easy text was one the child had read successfully in the past (or one very like it), an instructional text was one already introduced to the child so that he was somewhat familiar with the message and meanings of the story but had to engage in reading work and problem solving to read the text at the required accuracy level (90 percent or above), and the hard book may have been introduced or may be an unseen text one suspects the child will read less well and with which he will have some difficulty reaching the 90 percent accuracy level. The reason for using a ''seen'' text for the instructional level record is that we want to observe how well the reader orchestrates the various kinds of reading behaviors s/he controls, given that his/her reading is being guided by the meaningfulness of the text. The ''seen'' text ensures that the child understands the messages of the text and that meaningfulness will guide the reading.

This assumes there is some gradient of difficulty in the texts used for reading in the school's program, even if the children are learning to read from storybooks. The current book (or a selection from that book) will usually provide the instructional level. These three samples on three levels of difficulty provide valuable insights into

- how the reader orchestrates effective reading (on the easier materials)
- how processing and problem solving can be done (on instructional texts)

- how and when effective processing breaks down (on the more difficult materials).

The classroom teacher will probably choose text materials that are part of his/her everyday program. A visitor to the school (such as a reading adviser, a speech therapist, or a school psychologist) should ask the class teacher for the book the child is working on at present and for his/her suggestions about texts that are just a little harder or easier in his/her program.

If there are reasons why such judgments are not easily made—for example because the class does not use any recognizably graded sets of materials, or a teacher new to this class level has no sense of a gradient of difficulty in the stories being read—then the teacher or observer may wish to use a standard set of graded paragraphs. From these, the observer can select paragraphs that provide evidence of reading skills on three levels of difficulty to reveal strengths, processing skills, and weaknesses.

"Entonces lo cuidaré yo misma,"
dijo la gallinita roja.
Y así fue.
Todo el verano ella cuidó
el trigo crecido.
Se aseguró de que tuviese agua,
y arrancaba las malas hierbas
cuidadosamente de entre las hileras.
Al fin del verano el trigo había crecido.

From *La Gallinita Roja*, illustrated by Lucinda McQueen. Reprinted courtesy of Scholastic, New York.

A running record of reading behavior.

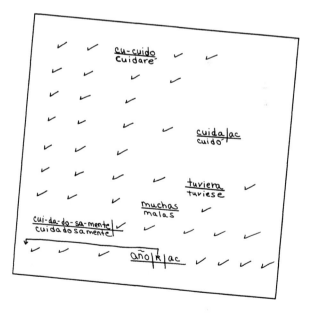

To take good records of reading behavior, teachers must be well trained. Six teachers taking and scoring the same record should get the same results; one teacher reading another teacher's record should be able to replay what a child actually said and did.

The running record on page 43 shows the child sampling and predicting (intelligently but incorrectly) *cuida* for *cuido*, and later self-correcting. Note that on *cuido* the child substituted one verb structure for another structure. Here the child was at first using a knowledge of syntactic as well as graphophonic cues. The child may have self-corrected when he noticed the accent mark.

LEARNING TO TAKE A RUNNING RECORD

Learning to take a running record can unsettle teachers. Those who are used to standardized tests and norms question the simplicity of the behavior records, and so do people who do not like standardized testing.

There is not a lot to learn before taking a running record—just a few conventions. There is no reason to study a new set of concepts or understand something new about the reading process. The first step is a matter of action. The teacher sets him/herself the task of recording everything a child says and does as s/he tries to read the book the teacher has chosen. Once such recording is begun, and after about two hours of initial practice, no matter how much might be missing, it is a good start. The more records a teacher makes the more s/he will notice about children's behavior. It is not a case of knowing everything first and then applying it. The more practice, the more is noticed. As a teacher's ear becomes tuned in to reading behaviors and s/he gains control over the recording conventions, the records will become more and more reliable.

Clay (1993) had been teaching reading and remedial reading for many years when she began research on emergent reading behavior. She was humbled by the fact that she had never noticed self-correction behavior until she started recording everything that children were doing. It was then she says that she found that she had been missing something that was very important.

What we are observing and recording is not something that is peculiar to the child who is learning to read. If we take some adult volunteers and ask them to read ordinary everyday reading materials, their reading behavior can be broken down so that we can observe the same kinds of behavior that occur in children's reading. A smudgy carbon copy, a poor FAX copy, a Churchill speech in initial teach-ing alphabet (a linguistics-based orthographic system for teaching English reading), a newspaper extract with misprints where the lines have been misplaced, or a very difficult scientific or medical text will break down the reading behaviors of competent adults and one can observe self-correction, word-by-word reading, and even the use of a pointing finger to locate themselves on the text. Everybody's reading behavior can be broken down according to difficulties—a phenomenon that is consistent across languages such as Spanish and English.

Each child's reading of his/her three little books or book selections should be recorded, using ticks (check marks) for each correct response and recording every error in full. A sample reading of one hundred to two hundred words from each text is required. This should take about ten minutes. At the early reading level when the child is reading the very simplest texts, the number of words may fall below one hundred, but if three texts are attempted (selected from caption books or first readers or teacher-made books or child-dictated text), this will be satisfactory even though the extracts themselves are short.

A suggested format for a Registro Progresivo *(Running Record Sheet)* can be found on pages 45–6 for Spanish and pages 47–8 for English. Procedures for calculating accuracy and self-correction rates are on page 66.

A teacher may choose to record Spanish running record data on an English running record sheet. Further, for bilingual teachers working with monolingual English principals or reading specialists, recording Spanish data on English forms may make them easier to interpret in the larger school and community environment. To maintain linguistic consistency, other teachers may prefer to record the information on a Spanish running record sheet. For that reason, running record sheets in both Spanish and English have been included in this book. Either one is acceptable to use in collecting and reading running record data in Spanish.

SOME CONVENTIONS USED FOR RECORDING

Numbers 1–11 below provide a description of each of the conventions for recording running record behaviors. Descriptions are provided in English with examples of student behavior in Spanish.

It is important to restate and reemphasize here that Spanish-speaking children living in the United States are in contact daily with print in two languages (English as well as Spanish). Although they may only be receiving

REGISTRO PROGRESIVO

Nombre _____ Fecha _____ Fecha de Nacimiento _____ Edad ____ Años ____ Meses ___

Escuela _____ Observador _____

Títulos del Texto	Palabras Actuales Error	Proporción de Errores	Exactitud	Proporción de Autocorrección
1. Fácil _____	_____	1: _____	_____%	1: _____
2. Requiere Enseñanza _____	_____	1: _____	_____%	1: _____
3. Difícil _____	_____	1: _____	_____%	1: _____

Movimiento Directivo _____

Análisis de Errores y de Autocorrecciones
Información utilizada o descuidada [Significado (S) Estructura o Sintaxis (E) Visual (V)]

Fácil _____

Requiere Enseñanza _____
_____

Difícil _____
_____

Cotejo de la Información (Observe que este comportamiento cambia con el tiempo)

_____   Análisis de Errores y de Autocorrecciones
_____   (ver *Instrumento de Observación*, páginas 54–55)

Página		E	AC	Información Utilizada E SEV	AC SEV

*Nivel de reto en el cual el niño puede beneficiarse de la enseñanza.

Página		E	AC	Información Utilizada	
				E SEV	AC SEV

RUNNING RECORD SHEET

Name: _____ Date: _____ D. of B.: _____ Age: _____ yrs _____ mths

School: _____ Recorder: _____

Text Titles		**Running words** **Error**	**Error rate**	**Accuracy**	**Self-correction** **rate**
1.	Easy _____	_____	1: _____	_____ %	1: _____
2.	Instructional _____	_____	1: _____	_____ %	1: _____
3.	Hard _____	_____	1: _____	_____ %	1: _____

Directional movement _____

Analysis of Errors and Self-corrections
Information used or neglected [Meaning (M) Structure or Syntax (S) Visual (V)]

Easy _____

Instructional _____

_____

Hard _____

_____

Cross-checking on information (Note that this behaviour changes over time)

_____

_____ Analysis of Errors and Self-corrections
(see *Observation Survey* pages 30–32)

Page		E	SC	Information used	
				E MSV	SC MSV

Page		E	SC	Information used	
				E MSV	SC MSV

formal reading instruction in Spanish in school, the print environment in school, outside the classroom, and in the larger community will often be in English. For this reason, many Spanish-speaking children engage in a linguistic behavior known as code-switching (the mixing of two languages). Among children learning two languages, code-switching has many forms and functions and often manifests itself in children's reading and writing as well as oral language.

For this reason, *El Instrumento de Observación* (Spanish Observation Survey) includes conventions for recording the reading behaviors of children who code-switch when they are reading Spanish text. Examples of noting and recording code-switching behaviors are included in numbers 12–14 below.

Recording conventions

1 Mark every word read correctly with a check or tick. A record of the first four lines of the book *La Margarita Friolenta* (1993) that was 100 percent correct would look like this. (The lines indicate page breaks.)

La Margarita Friolenta

Habiá una vez una margarita	✓ ✓ ✓ ✓ ✓
en un jardín.	✓ ✓ ✓
Cuándo cayó la noche,	✓ ✓ ✓ ✓
la margarita comenzó a temblar.	✓ ✓ ✓ ✓ ✓
En eso llegó volando	✓ ✓ ✓ ✓
una mariposa azul.	✓ ✓ ✓

2 Record a wrong response with the text under it.

Estudiante: cama
Texto: casa   [un error]

3 If a child tries several times to read a word, record all his trials.

Estudiante: m- | ma | mano
Texto: mano | | [no error]

Estudiante: cosa | ca | cama
Texto: casa | | [un error]

4 If a child succeeds in correcting a previous error this is recorded as "self-correction" (written SC in English; AC in Spanish for auto-corregido).

Estudiante: pato | pero | AC
Texto: perro | | [no error]

5 If no response is given to a word it is recorded with a dash. Insertion of a word is recorded over a dash.

No response: Insertion:

Estudiante: —   *Estudiante:* cosa
Texto: cosa   Texto: —   [en cada caso un error]

6 If the child balks, unable to proceed because he is aware he has made an error and cannot correct it or because he cannot attempt the next word, he is told or given the word recorded with a "T" (told) in English and a "D" (*dado la palabra*) in Spanish.

Estudiante: cama |
Texto: casa | D   [un error]

7 An appeal for help "A" (*ayuda*) in Spanish from the child is turned back to the child for further effort before using D as in 6 above. Say "Trátalo tú" ("*You try it*").

Estudiante: — | A | cosa
Texto: casa | — | D   [un error]

8 Sometimes the child gets into a state of confusion, and it is necessary to extricate him. The most detached method of doing this is to say "Trátalo otra vez" ("*Try that again*") marking TOV on the record. This would not involve any teaching, but the teacher may indicate where the child should begin again. It is a good idea to put brackets around the first set of muddled behavior, enter the "TOV," remember to count that as one error only (see p. 52) and then begin a fresh record of the problem text. An example of this recording would be:

Estudiante: [✓ | el | dice | la niña]
Texto: [Mamá | le | dijo | al niño] TOV

Estudiante: √ | el | R   AC | √ √ √
Texto: | le | |
[un error]

9 Repetition is not counted as error behavior. Sometimes it is used to confirm a previous attempt. Often it results in self-correction. It is useful to record it as it often indicates how much sorting out the child is doing. "R," standing for repetition (*repetir* in Spanish), is used to indicate repetition of a word, with R2 or R3 indicating the number of repetitions. If the child goes back over a group of words or returns to the beginning of the line or sentence in his/her repetition, the point to which s/he returns is shown by an arrow.

Estudiante: Mira   el   león | R | AC
Texto: Mira   el   tigre | | [no error]

10 Sometimes the child rereads the text (repetition) and corrects some but not all errors. The following example shows the recording of this behavior.

Estudiante: una | AC | muchachita   R
Texto: la | | niña | [un error/ un AC]

11 Directional attack on the printed text is recorded by telling the child "Leélo con tu dedo" *(Read it with your finger)*.

Left to right   L ⟶ R
Right to left   L ⟵ R
Snaking
Bottom to top B ⟶ T

Code-switching behaviors

The reader will note that Items 12–14 contain special conventions developed for this Spanish survey because it is intended for use in the United States where the majority of Spanish-speaking children are also exposed to English for a significant amount of their daily lives. Clay (1993) encourages teachers or researchers with special purposes such as those listed above to develop their own conventions for scoring other behaviors they notice. Some behaviors may be specific to, or important for, a particular teaching program such as a Spanish/English bilingual program.

12 Sometimes children use meaning cues from the English language at the same time they are using structure cues from the Spanish language. This is one type of code-switching behavior discussed above. The following is an example of this type of behavior.

Estudiante: √ | √ | √ | purple
Texto: tiene | un | sombrero | morado
[un error]

In the above example, the student used the meaning cue from the English language to get the word *purple* and the structure of the Spanish language in which a noun precedes an adjective.

13 Sometimes children use both meaning and structure cues from English and apply them to the Spanish reading situation at the same time that they are using structure and meaning cues from Spanish. This type of code-switching behavior is demonstrated in the following example.

Estudiante: √ | √ | purple | sombrero
Texto: tiene | un | sombrero | morado
[dos errores]

In the above example, the child used meaning and structure cues from Spanish to read the words *tiene* (present tense verb in the third person) and *un* (masculine indefinite article to match *sombrero*) as well as meaning and structure words from English to read the words *purple* and *sombrero*. In this case, the child used the English structure of adjective before noun when reading *purple sombrero*.

14 A third type of code-switching behavior involves using meaning from English and structure and visual cues from Spanish. This type of behavior is illustrated in the following example.

Estudiante: √ | √ | √ | red
Texto: tiene | un | sombrero | rojo [un error]

In this case the child used meaning from English (red) and structural and visual cues from Spanish (noun before adjective and visual structure of the word *rojo*).

For special purposes teachers or researchers may wish to develop their own conventions for scoring other behaviors they notice. Some behaviors may be specific to, or important for, a particular teaching program. For example, pausing can be recorded by a slash /. Some researchers who have been concerned with the length of pausing have used a convention borrowed from linguistics that allows for pauses of four different lengths. These are quickly recorded as

/   //   ‑++‑   **#**.

Clay (1993) cautions against attention to pausing unless there is a special reason for wishing to record it. *In research studies it has not yet yielded clear messages about the reading process* (Clay and Imlach 1971). It adds little to the teacher's interpretation of his/her record and may cause confusion. Pausing behavior is sensitive to the instructional program and may have been induced by the ways in which children are being taught. Pauses do not necessarily mean that "reading work" (as discussed in Clay 1991) is taking place. *It would be important not to read things into a record of pausing interpretations for which there was no other evidence.*

A running record from a child who is making many errors is harder to keep and to score, but the rule is to record all behavior and to analyze objectively what is recorded.

Reliability

Clay (1993) used taped recordings of running record reading observations taken from four children over the period of one year to establish reliability. These recordings were available and were used to check on the reliability of such records (0.98 for error scoring and 0.68 for self-correction scoring [Clay 1966]).

A number of trends became obvious during these reliability tests, and were noted by Clay (1993). These are:

- For beginning readers, observers can take running records that give reliable accuracy scores with a small amount of training.
- The effect of poor observation is to reduce the number of errors recorded and increase the accuracy rate. As the observer's skill in recording at speed increases, so the error scores tend to rise.
- To record all error behavior in full, as against only tallying its occurrence, takes much more practice (but provides more evidence of the child's strategies).
- Observations for poor readers require longer training to reach agreement on scoring standards because of the complex error behavior.
- Information is lost in the taped observation, especially motor behavior and visual survey, but observation of vocal behavior tends to be improved.
- Reliability probably drops as reading accuracy level falls because there is more error behavior to be recorded in the same time span.

For research work, the most reliable records would be obtained by scoring an observation immediately following its manual recording and rechecking immediately with a taped observation.

Reliability for this task in Spanish is assumed since the same procedures and protocols established by Clay are utilized when the task is administered in Spanish.

ANÁLISIS ACTUAL DEL TEXTO (ANALYZING THE READING RECORD)

From the running record of reading behavior containing all the child's behavior on his current book, consider what is happening as the child reads.

Some conventions for scoring the records

In counting the number of errors, some arbitrary decisions must be made but the following have been found workable.

1 Credit the child with any correct or corrected words.

Estudiante:	a	la	casa
Texto:	por	la	pelota
Resultado:	X		X [dos errores]

2 There is no penalty for trials which are eventually correct.

Estudiante:	puso	pon	poner	AC
Texto:	poner			
Resultado:	—	—	√	[no error; un AC]

Estudiante:	quiero	que	quebró	quedó	AC
Texto:	quedó				
Resultado:	—	—	—	√	[no error; un AC]

3 Insertions add errors so that a child can have more errors than there are words in a line.

Estudiante:	El	pájarito	dijo	pío	pío pío
Texto:	El	perico	puede	hablar	
Resultado:	X	X	X	X	X [cinco errores]

4 However, the child cannot receive a minus score for a page. The lowest page score is 0.

5 *Omissions.* If a line or sentence is omitted each word is counted as an error. If pages are omitted (perhaps because two pages were turned together), they are not counted as errors. Note that in this case, the number of words on the omitted pages must be deducted from the Running Words Total before calculation.

6 *Repeated errors.* If the child makes an error (e.g., *run* for *ran* or *dice* for *dijo*) and then substitutes this word repeatedly, it counts as an error every time; but substitution of a proper name (e.g., *Mary* for *Molly* or *Juan* for *José*) is counted only the first time.

7 *Multiple errors and self-correction.* If a child makes two or more errors (e.g., reads a phrase wrongly) each word is an error. If s/he then corrects all these errors each corrected word is a self-correction.

8 *Broken words.* Where a word is pronounced as two words (e.g., *a/way* in English or *a/quí* in Spanish) even when this is backed up by pointing as if it were two words, this is regarded as an error of pronunciation, not as a reading error unless what is said is matched to a different word. Such things as *pitcher* for *picture* and *gonna* for *going to* are counted as correct in English as are *onde* for *donde* or *voya* for *voy a* in Spanish.

9 *Inventions defeat the system.* When the young child is creatively producing his own version of the story, the scoring system finally breaks down and the judgment "inventing" is recorded for that page, story or book.

10 *"Trátalo otra vez o Trátalo de nuevo" (Try that again).* When the child is in a tangle, this instruction, which does not involve teaching, can be given. It counts as one error and only the second attempt is scored (see p. 49).

11 *Fewest errors.* If there are alternate ways of scoring responses a general principle is to choose the method that gives the fewest possible errors as in B below.

A *Estudiante:* Fuimos a comprar pan

Texto:	Fui	a	la	tienda	a	comprar	p a n
Resultado:	X		X	X		X	X	X

[seis errores]

B *Estudiante:* Fuimos   a comprar p a n

Texto:	Fui	a	la	tienda	a	comprar	p a n
Resultado:	X		X	X	X			

[cuatro errores]

12 *Accents.* If child fails to accentuate the word according to the written accent, this would change the meaning of the written text and should count as one error.

$$\frac{quito}{quitó} \quad [un\ error]$$

13 *Syllabication.* Since Spanish is a regular language and highly consistent in its phoneme/grapheme relationship, children may begin to read by syllables. This behavior must be monitored very carefully as students begin to use more visual information. In order to indicate this type of behavior, we have set up situations that will better record what the child is doing in order to observe what the child is attending to in the reading process.

A Child syllabicates word then reads the word correctly.

$$\frac{ar\text{-}dor\ |\checkmark}{ardor} \qquad \frac{cír\text{-}cu\text{-}lo\ |\checkmark}{círculo} \qquad [no\ error]$$

B Child begins by syllabicating but realizes what the word is midway through the word and completes correctly.

$$\frac{re\text{-}co\text{-}gían}{recogían} \qquad \frac{so\text{-}la\text{-}mente}{solamente} \qquad [no\ error]$$

C Child begins by syllabicating, then goes back and reads the entire word.

$$\frac{de\ \text{-}\ ba\ |\checkmark}{debajo} \qquad \frac{es\text{-}pe\ |\checkmark}{espera} \qquad [no\ error]$$

D While reading correctly, child syllabicates a word, then goes back to the beginning of the line and repeats the line correctly including the word previously syllabicated.

$$\frac{\boxed{\checkmark\ \checkmark\ \checkmark\ \checkmark\ \checkmark\quad cír\text{-}cu\text{-}lo\ |\quad R\ |\checkmark}}{círculo} \qquad [no\ error]$$

In all these cases, the child seems to be orchestrating sources of information that include syllabication. If a child begins to approach print using only syllabication, fluency will be affected and the teacher should begin to see a pattern in the documentation of the running record. The example below may indicate this type of approach.

$$\frac{Mi\quad ma\text{-}má\quad es\text{-}tá\quad en\quad ca\text{-}sa}{Mi\quad mamá\quad está\quad en\quad casa}$$

It is clear to see that the child is approaching the text syllable by syllable, even high frequency words or text that is supported by meaning and structure. Only by observing the child in the reading of the text and by recording this behavior will the teacher be able to determine how the child is using syllabication in reading.

Check directional movement

A check on the visual survey being carried out by the reader is needed. Select a few lines of text during the reading and ask the child "Lea esta (página/parte) con tu dedo" *(Read this part/page) with your finger)*. A brief observation will suffice, if all is well. More use of pointing should be observed if this is necessary (for the observer to understand what the child is doing). While pointing may not be a desirable teaching instruction, it is a necessary one for the observer to elicit evidence of directional movement. Record which hand was used, on which page, and the direction of movement.

In a study of children's early learning of directional movement across English texts, a common progression was noted (Clay 1982). There was an early period of confusion as the children tried to orient to the spatial characteristics of the open book. Then there was a period when the child seemed to prefer using a particular hand for pointing to any text. Finally a more flexible set of behaviors emerged when the child could use either hand on either page without having to pay much attention to direction. As these stages were worked through, sometimes rapidly and sometimes over several months, lapses from directional behaviors were observed. Children might go from right to left or even from bottom to top. Left-handed and right-handed children showed similar kinds of behaviors.

Three groups of children have difficulty as beginning readers in disciplining their behavior within the directional constraints of written language.

- The first group are children who have poor motor coordination or who are inattentive to where their bodies are and how they are arranging their movements.
- The second group are fast-reacting, impulsive children who act before they think and who have great difficulty in governing their responses within any constraints. They can very readily settle into undesirable patterns of responding.
- A third group of beginners at risk are those who do not like to try because they might make a mistake.

The development of directional behavior involves exploring two-dimensional space and discovering how to behave correctly within the constraints of the printer's code. Children need to be risk-takers. Children who are too tense, inhibited or timid, or afraid to be wrong may be reluctant to try out a range of directional behavior. Consequently they take longer to learn to discard the poor responses and retain the good ones.

The technique of saying to a child, "Leálo con tu dedo" *(Read it with your finger)* will only reveal directional behavior on the gross schema of line scanning. Beyond this there is some very important visual perception learning to be done. It relates to the scanning of letters and clusters of letters. There are further important orientation behaviors to be learned that involve what the eyes are attending to and in what order. These orientation behaviors will not be picked up in observations of pointing behavior.

Record your observations and comments on directional movement on your Registro Progresivo (pp. 45–6) or your Running Record Sheet (pp. 47–8). Any lapse from appropriate directional behavior is important and should be noted. We are not concerned merely with the child who habitually moves in the wrong direction, but rather with the child who is not yet consistent or, in other words, is still in the process of learning directional control. This is shown by lapses from correct directional behavior from time to time.

Calculate the error rate

Compare the number of errors with the number of running words. Does the child read his/her book with one error in every five running words of text (which is not good) or is it more like one error in twenty running words (which is good)? Record results on the Registro Progresivo Sheet or on the Running Record Sheet.

Calculate the percentage of errors (see Conversion Table p. 66). If there is more than a 10 percent error in the record rate this is a "hard" text for this child. (For the average child there is movement from 90 percent accuracy when s/he is first promoted to a book to 95 percent or more as s/he completes his/her learning on that book.)

When children read a book with less than 90 percent accuracy it is difficult for them to judge for themselves whether their attempts at a word are good ones or poor ones. They need easier material that they can attempt at a rate of not more than one error in ten words at the time they begin the new book. The reading text should use language that they can easily anticipate. In the very earliest stages it is sometimes necessary to repeat the text until children have almost memorized it, but not quite. Then it will come readily to the tip of the tongue. It is as if the words the child needs are stored in the depths of memory and have to be assisted to float to the surface. The child's own dictated stories provide good reading texts for young children for just this reason—the words and construction of the text should be readily recalled.

If the text is in a different style from that which the child usually reads, his/her error rate may increase because s/he is predicting from the baseline of old expectations that are inappropriate for the present text.

Error behavior: What can we learn from this?

To read a continuous text the child must use a variety of skills held in delicate balance. Specific weaknesses or strengths can upset that balance. There are some questions about the errors for a particular child that can guide the teacher's analysis of the behavior record (see also Clay 1991). At this point attend only to the errors (and not the self-corrections).

Oral language skills
Are these good enough to make the reading of this text possible? (For instance, could the child repeat the sentence tenses of the text if you asked her/him to, one by one?) Or, is his/her language so fluent that the coordination of visual perception and motor movement with language is difficult?

Speed of responding
The rate at which a child reads and the time spent on pausing and processing cues are poor indicators of progress in the young child. One child may read with the fluency of oral language but may be a poorer reader than another child who pauses and engages in much self-correction behavior. At this particular stage in reading progress it is good for the child making average progress to be concerned about errors and try to rectify errors if possible. It is poor to maintain fluency and not notice that one has made errors.

Fast responding can be an indication that language is dominating the reading process allowing for little visual search to take place.

What kinds of information does the child use?
To work out whether the child is responding to the different sources of information in print (and the different kinds of cues that could be used) the teacher needs to look at every error the child makes and ask, "Now what led the child to do (or say) that?" The teacher needs to determine whether the child was using information from:

* the meaning of the message
* the structure of the sentence
* something from the visual cues.

Firstly, the teacher considers only the behavior up to the error.

* Sentido/Significado (*Meaning*). Does the child use meaning (M in English—S in Spanish)? If what s/he reads makes sense, even though it is inaccurate, then s/he is probably applying his/her knowledge of the world to his/her reading.
* Estructura (*Structure*). Is what s/he said possible in a Spanish sentence (E for syntactically appropriate in Spanish; S in English)? If it is, his/her oral language is probably influencing his/her responding. If it is not, there may be two reasons. Perhaps his/her language skill is limited and his/her personal grammar does not contain the structures used in his/her reading book. Or, if s/he is paying close attention to detail, or to word-by-word reading, s/he may not be allowing his/her control over English/Spanish syntax to influence his/her choices.
* Visual (*Visual formation*). Does s/he use visual information (V in either Spanish or English) from the letters and words or the layout of print?*
* Memoria de palabras (*Word memory*). Does s/he read word by word as if recalling each word from a memory bank, unrelated to what has gone before? S/he may not realize that reading is like speaking and that his/her language behavior is a rich source of help in choosing correct reading responses.

It is misleading if the teacher looks for error behavior selectively; one should analyze every error and count those that show attention to this or that kind of cue. We want to be able to conclude, on good evidence, that "s/he pays more attention to visual cues than to meaning," or "s/he is guided by structure and meaning but does not search for visual cues." It is only when the teacher goes to the trouble of analyzing all the errors that

*Whether the child is relating visual information to sounds (phonological information) or to orthography (information about spelling) is a refinement of using visual information not distinguished in this analysis at this time.

s/he gets quality information about the way the reader is working on print.

When teachers are familiar with registros progresivos *(taking running records)*, they may want to include error analysis on the record form. They can write **S** for meaning *(sentido/significado)*, **E** for structure *(estructura)*, and **V** for visual cues *(señales visuales)* on the form and record, by circling which cues the child was using. (See Registro Progresivo, pp. 45–6 or the Running Record Sheet, pp. 47–8.) To notice that what one is recording in this case is one's best guess: the teacher cannot know what cues the child used. A record may show one, two, or three types of cues used on any one error. If the teacher writes SEV alongside each error and circle the cues s/he thinks the child used, the uncircled letters will then show the cues neglected.

The teacher has considered the errors first and knows what cues *up to that error* the child was using. Comments are to be on the Análisis de Errores y Actos de Auto-Corregir (Registro Progresivo) in Spanish or Analysis of Errors and Self-corrections (Running Record Sheet in English).

Cross-checking strategies

The next step to consider is whether the child can check one kind of information with another.

Cross-checking is a tentative behavior. It is not possible to be specific about it. One has a hunch that it is happening after observing the child. We must ask, "Is this child checking one kind of information against another?"

Cross-checking is most obvious when a child is not satisfied with a response for some reason. S/he may make another attempt, or look back, or think again, or complain that a necessary letter is missing. Usually two sources of information are involved, and one is checked against the other.

The child checks on the word which s/he read using one kind of information by looking at a different kind of information. S/he uses meaning but complains that some letters are not there. S/he uses visual cues from letters but says that it doesn't make sense.

Some examples of this kind of behavior are:

- S/he can get both movement and language occurring together in a coordinated way and knows when s/he has run out of words.
- S/he checks language prediction by looking at some letters.

- S/he can hear the sounds in a word s/he speaks and checks whether the expected letters are there.
- After a wrong response a child can make another attempt at the word (searching).
- After a wrong response the child repeats the sentence, phrase, or word, indicating s/he is aware that an error has been made and is trying to get some additional information (repeating).
- After a wrong response the child makes a verbal comment about it, for example, "No! That's not right!" (commenting on the mismatch).

It is useful to try to specify which two kinds of information the child is comparing. Usually cross-checking is reserved for describing early behaviors that suggest the child knows there are different kinds of information in print and that one kind can be compared with another kind and that s/he expects all kinds to agree on the solution. Most of this behavior becomes superseded by more deliberate and successful attempts to self-correct using multiple sources of information.

A child with outstanding memory for what he hears or with very fast language production often has difficulty in slowing up enough to enable him/her to learn the visual discriminations. Yet good readers search for cues from different sources to confirm a response. (See pp. 11–13 and Clay 1991 for further discussion of these reading behaviors.)

Self-correction

These procedures are to be followed in looking at any self-correction behavior in the running record. This occurs when the child discovers information in the text that tells him/her something is wrong. S/he is aware that a particular message is to be communicated and tries to discover this by using cues. Efficient self-correction behavior is an important skill in good reading. Calculate the self-correction rate (see p. 66). Even if the self-correction rate is low the prognosis is good, because self-correction does exist!

When analyzing self-corrections for the information they can give about the child's processing of print, consider the error first. What kind of information was the child using up to the time when the error occurred? Think only of the information in the error substitution. Then, in a two-step process, consider what extra information the child used to get the self-correction. What extra information is in the self-correction that was not in the error? Enter on the Registro Progresivo or on the Running Record Sheet in the second of the analysis columns headed AC (auto-corregir) in Spanish or SC (self-correction) in English. Include all the sources of information probably being used in the self-correction. Write SEV in Spanish or MSV in English alongside each self-correction and circle the cues you think the child used. Are cross-checking strategies evident in the self-correction analysis?

If self-correction is evident but inefficient, it is still a good prognosis. Its absence in a record that contains errors is a danger sign. A child who is making errors and is not aware of it, or who makes no attempt to correct him/herself, is in difficulty. S/he is not aware of the need to read a precise message or s/he is not aware of the existence of cues, or s/he does not know how to use them, or s/he does not try to solve the problem. Self-correction rates vary greatly. This is because they are not absolute scores: they are always relative measures. They vary with text difficulty, with error rate, with accuracy, and with effort. They cannot be understood unless they are interpreted together with text difficulty and accuracy scores.

Examples of self-correcting behaviors in Spanish

I Linda and Jasmíne were reading the book that gave rise to the example of reading behaviors in English on page 57 and in Spanish on page 58. (It was not a very helpful book for their level of reading and it was a "contrived text" [Clay 1991] using controlled vocabulary.) You might think that they were poor readers. Yet when you think about what is going on in these records, how many things they are trying to do, and what kinds of cues they are testing out, you can see that they really are working hard to relate one kind of information to another. This is a very interesting record of behavior, showing how active they are in searching and checking. In time they must become more efficient at doing these things.

II The next example comes from a child who was able to engage in finding and correcting her own errors as she read, almost independently, with very little assistance from her teacher.

The teacher listened as the child read one or two self-chosen, easy books. The teacher said "Leélo con tu dedo." *(Read it with your finger.)*

"Ahora sí salió bien," *(Now it came out right)*, the child said. "Tuve bastante palabras cada vez que apunté." *(I had enough words for each one I pointed to.)*

The teacher offered no assistance as the child reread

the book they had worked on together in a previous lesson. They continued with the reading until the child, puzzled, stopped. (The teacher had said nothing.)

"No tiene sentido," *(It doesn't make sense)* , the child observed, repeating the beginning of the sentence, taking another look. Then, after a moment, the child reflected aloud, "Oh, es 'aquí'. Ahora sí tiene sentido." *(Oh, the word is aquí. Now it makes sense.)*

A little later the child shook her head and seemed uncertain.

The teacher asked, "¿Por qué paraste?" *(Why did you stop?)*

"No me acuerdo de la palabra" *(I don't remember the word)*, said the child.

"¿Qué palabra tiene sentido aquí?" *(What word makes sense here?)*, asked the teacher.

"Moto. Pero esta palabra es más larga. Tiene que ser moto. ¡Oh! es motocicleta." *(Moto. But this word is longer. It has to be moto. Oh! It's motorcycle.)*

Keeping records of change over time

Education is primarily concerned with change in the learning of individuals, yet educators rarely document change over time in individuals as they grow and learn. Perhaps the diversity among individuals in all characteristics from height to habits to school achievements clouds the progress that each makes. But it is not difficult to collect evidence of change over time in school learning, particularly from young children at the beginning of formal education.

Two ways of recording individual progress over time in running records are shown below.

In Adriana's case the teacher grouped her books into approximate levels of difficulty for each child. She placed these numbers on the left side of her sheet. Then, when she took her running records of Adriana's reading on two occasions several months apart, she entered in the name of the story Adriana read and whether this story was easy, instructional, or hard for her.

In Miguel's case, his teacher was keeping a very close record of his progress. This time the teacher used graph paper. She entered the level of book difficulty on the left and entered the date of the observation along the horizontal line for the weekly observations she was taking. After hearing Miguel read his current book, she entered an open circle at the level of the one she considered him to be reading at an "instructional" level (at 90 to 94 percent accuracy level). If no story was read at this level or better, the teacher had evidence

AN EXAMPLE OF VERY COMPLICATED WORD-SOLVING AND SELF-CORRECTION BEHAVIOUR

Response to: **I like the swing. I shall get on it. The swing went up and down. It went . . .**	INTERPRETATION OF BEHAVIOUR		
	TRIES	DECIDES	REASONS
I like the swing	Correct		
I shall ke — get	Anticipates wrongly	Corrects	Letter cue?
off it — on it	Anticipates wrongly	Corrects	Meaning?
The swing will — No!	First letter cue	Rejects	Word form?
wa — want	Three letters similar	Rejects	Meaning?
won't (up) — No!	Structure cue 'The swing won't . . .' plus three letters	Rejects	Following structure 'won't up'?
will take	New idea	Rejects	One pattern for two responses
we — wa — No	A more analytical approach	Rejects	Sounds do not aid recall
(I get mixed up)		'I am confused'	There is always some cue that does not fit
(I'll read it again)	A new approach	Return to the line beginning	'A clean slate'
The swing want	It looks like 'want'	Rejects	Meaning?
won't up and down	It looks like 'won't'	Accepts	Fits letter and meaning cues and previous structure
It — (I get mixed up)	Recognises the same word	I am confused. Start again.	
It won't	Tries previous solution	Rejects	
went?	Tries correct sound 'e'	I do not recognise this word	There has been too much error
(I don't know that word)	Gives up	Appeals for help	No more ideas

that she had been making the task too difficult for Miguel's current competencies and entered a filled or black circle to alert herself to her own error. Miguel's record is a good one. Whenever his teacher raises the challenge by introducing a more difficult text, Miguel is able to take the challenge and read at appropriate levels of accuracy.

A teacher may follow several children in this way, even though they are taught separately, using the same plotting procedures she used for Miguel but entering all the children on the one graph. This will not only give her a record of progress but also show many things about individual differences

- in the starting levels
- in the paths of progress
- in fast or slow "take-off" in her program
- in final or outcome levels.

AN EXAMPLE OF VERY COMPLICATED WORD-SOLVING AND SELF-CORRECTION BEHAVIOR

Me gusta el columpio. Me voy a pasear en él. El columpio subió alto y bajó rápido. Se subió. . .	INTERPRETATION OF BEHAVIOR		
	TRIES	DECIDES	REASONS
Me gusta el columpio	Correct		
Me do -- voy	Anticipates wrongly	Corrects	Letter cue?
a paseo - a pasear en él.	Anticipates wrongly	Corrects	Meaning?
El columpio sabe -- ¡No!	First letter cue	Rejects	Word form?
su -- subo	Three letters similiar	Rejects	Meaning?
sabía (alto) -- ¡No!	Structure cue El columpio sabía ... plus three letters	Rejects	Following structure '¿sabía alto?'
se va	New Idea	Rejects	One pattern for two responses
su -- *sa -- No*	A more analytical approach	Rejects	Sounds do not aid recall
(Me confundo)		'Me confundo'	There is always some cue that does not fit
(Lo voy a leer otra vez)	A new approach	Return to the line beginning	'Empezar de nuevo'
El columpio subo	Parece como 'subo'	Rejects	Meaning?
sabía alto y bajó rápido	Parece como 'sabia'	Accepts	Fits letter and meaning cues and previous structure
Se -- *(Me confundo)*	Recognizes the same word	'Me confundo'	
Se subo	Tries previous solution	Rejects	
subió	Tries correct sound 'ió'	'No sé esta palabra'	There has been too much error
(No sé la palabra)	Gives up	Appeals for help	No more ideas

She will be able to quickly identify any children who are working with texts that are too difficult for them, preventing them from working in the context of mostly correct reading (instructional level of 90 percent accuracy or above).

Next we have two examples of what a teacher could learn from her/his Running Record about how her/his pupils were trying to problem-solve text. Both records were taken in the first weeks of an early intervention program.

• Child one, in Spanish, (see *La Fruta* story) is paying some attention to sentence structure *(estructura)* and meaning because her errors all reflect the use of mean-

PROGRESO DE ADRIANA SOBRE TEXTOS
DOS PUNTOS DE OBSERVACIÓN

LIBRO NIVEL	Primera Vez	LIBRO NIVEL	Segunda Vez
9		. . .	
8		. . .	
7		18	
6		17	
5—*Las Estaciones*	(difícil)	16	
4—*Mi Ropa*	(instruccional)	15	
3— *Yo Amo a Mi Familia*	(fácil)	14	
2		13	
1		12—*Chana Y Su Rana*	(difícil)
0		11—*El Carrito De Monchito*	(instruccional)
		10—*Fue Carmelita*	(fácil)

ing and sentence structure in decision making. But she is not yet showing any awareness of a mismatch between her responses and the visual information of the text.

- Child two, in Spanish, (see *La Fruta* story) is paying some attention to visual information and structure in text for her decision making (*n* in *niño* is like *n* in *naranja*). However, with this error, she pays no attention to meaning. In the second set of errors, she also pays some attention to sentence structure and meaning, but in this case pays no attention to visual information in the text.

Calculation and conversion table

Whether children are reading seen or unseen texts, most of their reading will contain errors. This is fortunate because it allows teachers to observe how children work on texts to problem-solve and monitor their own reading.

The Conversion Table (p. 66) provides for a quick conversion of error rate to a percentage accuracy score. This allows teachers to offer children texts that provide the support of a meaningful context within which to do their problem solving.

Running records with older readers

Clay (1993) includes a discussion of the uses of Running Records in English with older students. These records with older students can be used to further analyze student literacy behaviors with text that is more difficult and with text that is expository as well as narrative in structure.

Running records with older readers enable teachers to continue to observe which strategies students are utilizing effectively and which still need to be more finely tuned. They are also useful in following the progress of students who have been in early literacy intervention programs such as Descubriendo La Lectura or Reading Recovery, and to monitor whether gains made in early literacy programs are sustained across grade levels after students leave these programs.

In Tucson, one researcher has been following a student for five years (Brena 1995). This student, named Blanca, entered kindergarten in 1990 speaking no English. Yet, because of parent request, she was placed in an all-English kindergarten. At the end of kindergarten, she had made little progress in English reading and writing and was simultaneously recommended for retention and/or special education. As a result of her slow progress and to avoid retention, her mother consented to placing her in a bilingual first grade classroom where her literacy program would be in Spanish. Her first grade teacher immediately recognized that Blanca needed "something extra" and recommended her for Descubriendo La Lectura. Her acceleration during her Descubriendo La Lectura program, combined with a classroom reading program in Spanish, was truly remarkable. She progressed from having few literacy strategies to being able to read a Spanish text at the second grade level with a 95 percent accuracy rate and a 1:2 self-correction rate when she discontinued the program in February 1992. By the end of the school year, she was reading text at a fourth grade level in Spanish with a 97 percent accuracy rate and a self-correction rate of 1:4.

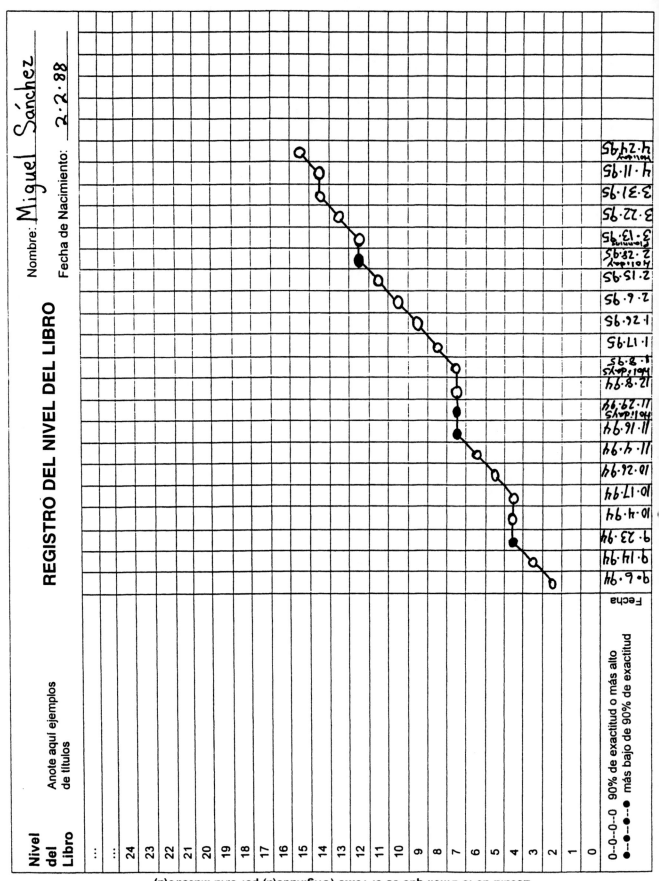

Nombre: Miguel Sánchez

Fecha de Nacimiento: 2.2.88

REGISTRO DEL NIVEL DEL LIBRO

Nivel del Libro

Anote aquí ejemplos de títulos

Escala de lo Difícil que es el Texto (Originado(a) por el/la Maestro(a))

Fecha

O—O—O—O 90% de exactitud o más alto
●—●—●—● más bajo de 90% de exactitud

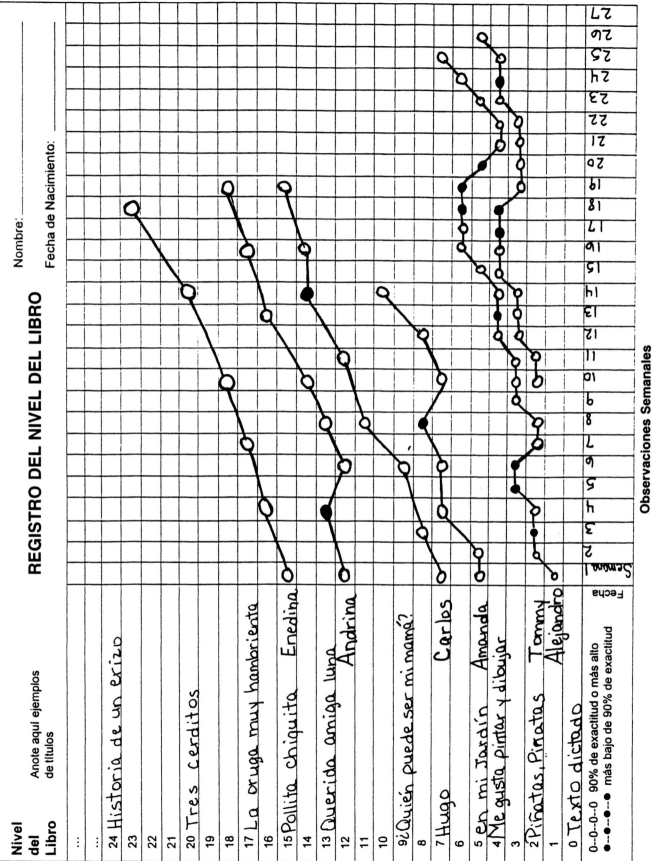

REGISTRO DEL NIVEL DEL LIBRO

Nombre: _____

Fecha de Nacimiento: _____

Nivel del Libro — Anote aquí ejemplos de títulos

:::	
:::	
24	Historia de un erizo
23	
22	
21	
20	Tres cerditos
19	
18	
17	La oruga muy hambrienta
16	
15	Pollita chiquita
14	
13	Querida amiga luna
12	
11	
10	
9	¿Quién puede ser mi mamá?
8	
7	Hugo
6	
5	En mi jardín
4	Me gusta pintar y dibujar
3	
2	Piñatas, Piñatas
1	
0	Texto dictado

Enedina
Andrina
Carlos
Amanda
Tommy
Alejandro

Semana
Fecha

Escala de lo Difícil que es el Texto (Originado(a) por el/la Maestro(a))

Observaciones Semanales

0–0–0–0 90% de exactitud o más alto
●—●—● más bajo de 90% de exactitud
● 90% de exactitud o más alto

RECORD OF BOOK LEVEL

Name: _____

Date of Birth: _____

Book Level	Enter examples of titles here
...	
...	
24	
23	
22	
21	
20	
19	
18	
17	
16	
15	
14	
13	
12	
11	
10	
9	
8	
7	
6	
5	
4	
3	
2	
1	
0	
Date	

Gradient of Text Difficulty (Teacher Devised)

o—o—o 90% accuracy or above

•—•—• below 90% accuracy

Weekly Observations

REGISTRO DEL NIVEL DEL LIBRO

Nombre: _____

Fecha de Nacimiento: _____

Nivel del Libro	Anote aquí ejemplos de títulos
...	
...	
24	
23	
22	
21	
20	
19	
18	
17	
16	
15	
14	
13	
12	
11	
10	
9	
8	
7	
6	
5	
4	
3	
2	
1	
0	

Fecha

0–0–0–0 90% de exactitud o más alto
●–●–●–● más bajo de 90% de exactitud

Escala de lo Difícil que es el Texto (Originado(a) por el/la Maestro(a))

Observaciones Semanales

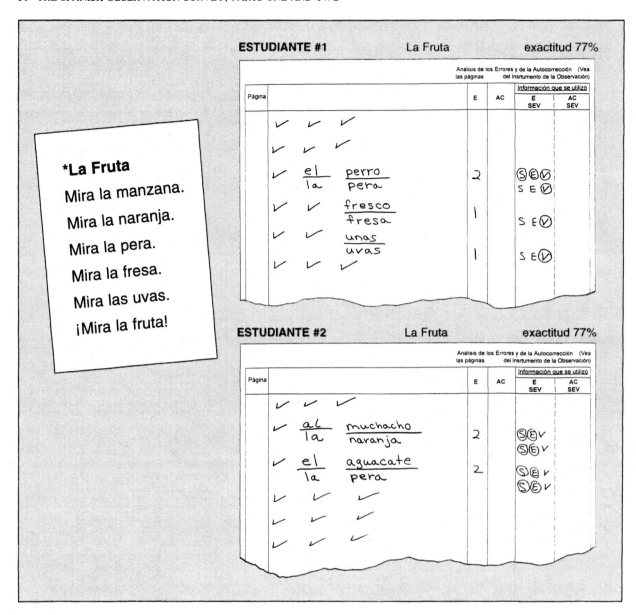

*La Fruta

Mira la manzana.

Mira la naranja.

Mira la pera.

Mira la fresa.

Mira las uvas.

¡Mira la fruta!

So intrigued was Brena with the progress that she decided to follow Blanca across grade levels to monitor her literacy progress in Spanish and to observe how this progress might transfer to reading in English. To do this, she utilized running records across grade levels utilizing both Spanish and English texts as well as narrative and expository selections.

The case study profile on page 67 illustrates Blanca's progress in literacy across first grade (when she was in Descubriendo La Lectura) and into second, third, and fourth grades when she had no special program in-struction, except for her regular bilingual education class. It is important to note that Blanca has continued to accelerate in Spanish reading and that her reading abilities are above grade level in Spanish for both narrative texts (the basic Spanish reading program) and expository texts in Spanish for social studies and science. Further, Blanca began the process of becoming biliterate in the third grade and running records of her reading behavior in English have demonstrated that she is also reading at grade level in English.

Many more of these case studies are currently being

A running record taken on the Running Record Sheet

REGISTRO PROGRESIVO

Nombre: **Sara** Fecha: **10-12-94** Fecha de Nacimiento: **5·21·88** Edad: **6** años **5** meses

Escuela: **Manzo** Observador: **O. R.**

Títulos del Texto	Palabras Actuales Errores	Proporción de Errores	Exactitud	Proporción de la Autocorrección
1. Fácil		1:	%	1:
2. Requiere Enseñanza		1:	%	1:
3. Difícil **Me gusta pintar y dibujar** (familiar)	**46/6**	1: **7.6**	**87.5** %	1: **3**

Movimiento directivo

Análisis de Errores y de Autocorrección

Información utilizada o descuidada [Significado (S) Estructura (E) Visual (V)]

Fácil

Requiere Enseñanza

Difícil **Predomina el uso de claves de significado y estructura al reemplazar palabras con un poco de atención a claves visuales.**

Cotejo de la información. (Observe que este comportamiento cambia con el tiempo)
En tres ejemplos parece que las claves de significado y estructura fueron comprobadas con claves visuales

Análisis de Errores y de Autocorrección (Vea las páginas 54–55 del *Instrumento de la Observación*)

Página		E	AC	Información utilizada E SEV	AC SEV
2.	✓ ✓ ✓ ✓ ventana/ac ___ casa		1	(S)(E)V	S E (V)
3.	✓ ✓ pintar ✓ ratón ___ dibujar ratoncito	2		(S)(E)V (S)(E)(V)	
4.	✓ ✓ ✓ ✓ ✓				
5.	✓ ✓ pintar ___ dibujar	1		(S)(E)V	
6.	✓ ✓ ✓ ✓ ✓				
7.	✓ ✓ ✓ ✓ f- [R] ___ frasco [D]	1		S E (V)	
8.	✓ ✓ pintar [R]/ac ✓ ✓		1	(S)(E)V	S E (V)
9.	✓ ✓ pintar/ac ✓ pared ___ dibujar ciudad	1	1	(S)(E)V (S)(E)V	S E (V)
10	✓ ✓ ✓ ✓ ✓				
11.	Payaso ___ Píntame	1		(S)(E)(V)	
		6	3	8 7 3	0 0 3

CONVERSION TABLE

Proporción de Errores *(Error Rate)*	Porcentaje de Exactitud *(Percent Accuracy)*	Comentarios *(Comments)*
1 : 200	99.5	
1 : 100	99.0	
1 : 50	98.0	
1 : 35	97.0	
1 : 25	96.0	Good opportunities for teachers
1 : 20	95.0	to observe children's "reading
1 : 17	94.0	work."
1 : 14	93.0	
1 : 12.5	92.0	
1 : 11.75	91.0	
1 : 10	90.0	
1 : 9	89.0	
1 : 8	87.5	
1 : 7	85.5	The reader tends to lose
1 : 6	83.0	the support of the
1 : 5	80.0	meaning of the text
1 : 4	75.0	
1 : 3	66.0	
1 : 2	50.0	

CALCULACIONES *(CALCULATIONS)*

(PA = Palabras actuales - *Running words;* E = Errores - *Errors;* AC = Auto-corregir - *Self-corrections);* Porcentaje de Exactitud - *Accuracy)*

PROPORCIÓN DE ERRORES	PORCENTAJE DE EXACTITUD	PROPORCIÓN DE AUTO-CORREGIR
$\dfrac{\text{Palabras actuales}}{\text{Errores}}$ e.g. $\dfrac{150}{15}$ = Proporción 1:10	$100 - \dfrac{E}{PA} \times \dfrac{100}{1}$ $100 - \dfrac{15}{150} \times \dfrac{100}{1}$ = 90 porcentaje	$\dfrac{E + AC}{AC}$ $\dfrac{15 + 5}{5}$ = Proporción 1:4

conducted on bilingual students while they are in Descubriendo La Lectura programs and after they discontinue them. Running records are key tools not only in collecting data on initial student reading behaviors, but also on their behaviors as they continue to develop across grade levels.

DESCUBRIENDO LA LECTURA / CASE STUDY PROFILE
BLANCA

	First Grade			Second Grade		Third Grade	
	1991–92			1992–93		1993–94	1994–95
	PRE	POST	END OF YEAR	PRE	POST		
(Identificación de Letras) *Letter Identification*	26/61	54/61	*	60/61	*	*	*
(Prueba de Palabras) *Tucson Word Test*	0/20	19/20	*	19/20	*	*	*
(Conceptos del Texto Impreso) *Concepts About Print*	6/241	6/24	*	17/24	*	*	*
(Escritura de Vocabulario) *Writing Vocabulary*	3	44	*	40	43	*	*
(Dictado) *Dictation*	8/39	36/39	34/39	37/39	39/39	74/74	*
(Lectura de Textos) *Text Reading*	A	L 18–95% SC 1:2 Gr. 2 Spanish	L 26–97% SC 1:4 Gr. 4 Spanish	L 17–94% SC 1:4 GRADE 2	L 30–98% SC 1:2 GRADE 6 1st Gr. English L 9–99% SC 1:1	*5th Gr. Span.* **Houghton-Mifflin** *(Banderas)* **94% / SC 1:3** *6th Gr. Span.* *(Portales)* **90% / SC 1:2** *3rd Gr. English* **Houghton-Mifflin 95% / SC 1:6**	*6th Gr. Span.* *(Portales)* **97% / SC 1:4** *(Science)* **95% / SC 1:NIL** *(Social Studies)* **100% / SC 1:NIL** *4th Gr. English* **Houghton-Mifflin 98% / SC 1:3 96% / SC 1.8**

*Certain subtests of the Observation Survey were not administered.

7
OTRAS TAREAS
DE OBSERVACIÓN
(Other Observation Tasks)

Kathy Escamilla
Ana María Andrade
Amelia G. M. Basurto
with Marie Clay

The reader may wish to refer back to pages 39–40 of the general introduction to the observation survey before reading Chapter 7, noting in particular the warning that no one task is satisfactory as an assessment on its own.

IDENTIFICACIÓN DE LETRAS
(LETTER IDENTIFICATION)

Briefly stated, the purpose of this observation task is to distinguish letters one from another on any basis that works. This task enables a teacher to observe such things as which letters the child knows and which ones s/he can identify. It is not sufficient to say that s/he knows "a few letters." It is important to take into account exactly what s/he knows. (This observation task should take five to ten minutes.)

Administration

Test all letters, lower case and upper case. The large print alphabet on the page 70 should be used. It could be copied or removed from the book and mounted on a clipboard for this purpose. Ensure that the child reads *across* the lines so that the letters are treated in a random, not alphabetical, order.

Use only the following questions to get the child to respond to the letters. *Do not ask only for sounds or names.*

Para presentar la tarea *(To introduce the task)*:
- ¿Qué son éstas? (*What do you call these?*)
- ¿Puedes encontrar algunas que tú conoces? (*Can you find some that you know?*)

Enseñando cada letra *(Pointing to each letter in horizontal lines)*:
- ¿Qué es ésta? (*What is this one?*)

Si el niño no responde *(If a child does not respond)*:
Use una o más de estas preguntas y trate de evitar preferencia hacia una u otra (*Use one or more of these questions and try to avoid bias toward any one of them*).

- ¿Sabes el nombre de la letra? (*Do you know its name?*)
- ¿Qué sonido tiene? (*What sound does it make?*)
- ¿Sabes una palabra que empieza así? (*Do you know a word that starts like that?*)

Para ñ y rr, se dice *(for ñ and rr, you say)*:
- ¿Sabes una palabra que tiene ese sonido? (*Do you know a word that has this sound?*)

Enseñando otras letras *(Then moving to other letters)*:
- ¿Qué es ésta? (*What is this?*)
- ¿Y ésta, qué es? (*And this, what is it?*)

If the child hesitates, start with the first letter of his/her name and then go to the first line. Point to every letter in turn working across the lines. Use a masking card if necessary.

Scoring the record

The following are suggested guidelines for scoring this task. Use la Resultados De La Identificación de Letras (*Letter Identification Score Sheet*) included on page 71 to help you.

- Mark column *A* for an alphabetical response *(respuesta con nombre alfabética).*
- Mark column *S* with a checkmark for a response that represents a letter sound *(respuesta con el sonido que hace la letra)* or if the student responds with a syllable, write in the syllable response *(respuesta de sílaba).*
- Mark column *P* if the response was for a word beginning similarly and write the word *(respuesta de una palabra que empieza con la letra, y anote la palabra que dice el niño/la niña).*
- If the child responded with the correct letter or sound in English, mark the appropriate column with a checkmark and an *E.*
- If the child responded with a word beginning with the letter in English, (e.g., *Superman* for *S* or *Q-tip* for *Q*), write the English word that the child says under the word column.
- For incorrect responses record what the child says under the column *RI (respuesta incorrecta).*

Score as correct:

- Respuesta con nombre alfabética *(an alphabet name)*
- Sonido de la letra *(a sound that is acceptable for that letter)*
- Palabra—una respuesta que dice "...empieza como. ..." dando una palabra por cual la letra es la letra inicial *(a response which says "... it begins like ..." giving a word for which that letter is the initial letter)*
- Inglés *(English)*—a response in English using the name, sound, or word that is correct.

In addition, the following scoring conventions are suggested for letters that exist in Spanish but not in English. In these cases, further prompting is suggested to determine if the child can identify these letters as units.

- *Ll/ll* can be identified as *elle* or *doble L*. Either is a correct response. A response such as *ele-ele* is not acceptable alone and requires further prompting to see if the child recognizes the letter as a unit.
- *Ch/ch* can be identified as *che.*
- *rr* can be identified as *erre* or *doble r*. Either is a correct response. A response such as *ere-ere* is not acceptable alone and requires further prompting to see if the child recognizes the letter as a unit.
- *H/h* can also be identified as *muda.*
- *rr* and *N/ñ* are the exceptions for accepting the middle sound in words as correct responses (e.g., *perro—niño*).
- Regional variations are acceptable. If clarification is needed prompt further.

The scores given below apply when any one of these four criteria is used to mark a response correct. Obtain subtotals for each kind of response—alphabetical, sound, word beginning similarly, or English response—and note down for the record as a whole:

- the child's preferred mode of identifying letters
- the letters a child confuses, so that they can be kept apart in the teaching program
- the unknown letters.

Interpretation of scores

Tables that follow each observation task in this chapter show scores as stanine scores for two large samples of children. For comparison choose the research group that best represents the group of children you will be testing. Choose the first table if you are assessing children at the beginning of first grade (fall). A stanine score of 5 seems to fit with average progress in your school. Choose the second table if you are assessing children at the end of first grade (spring). It is also useful for a school to build up its own table of stanine scores (see Lyman 1963, Clay 1993).

Stanines distribute scores according to the normal curve in nine groups from 1 (a low score) to 9 (a high score) (see Lyman 1963). They are normalized standard scores. Stanines can be used for normative test purposes to compare pupils one with another and an individual child with a group of children. But a more important reason for using stanines is to compare an individual child's progress across various tests that have different ranges of scores (i.e., when raw scores are not comparable). They allow one pupil's progress to be compared on several quite different types of observations. Following such testing, teaching should aim to improve the child's ability to distinguish letters one from another on any basis

A	F	K	P	Ll	Z
B	H	O	J	U	Ch
C	Y	L	Q	M	Ñ
D	N	S	X	I	E
G	R	V	T	W	
a	f	k	p	ll	z
b	h	o	j	u	ch
c	y	l	q	m	ñ
d	n	s	x	i	a
e	g	r	v	t	w
rr	g				

RESULTADOS DE LA IDENTIFICACIÓN DE LETRAS

Resultado

/61

Fecha:_____

Nombre:_____ Escuela:_____ Grado: _____

Maestra/o de clase:_____ Observador:_____

	A	S	Palabra	R.I.		A	S	Palabra	R.I.
A					a				
F					f				
K					k				
P					p				
Ll					ll				
Z					z				
B					b				
H					h				
O					o				
J					j				
U					u				
Ch					ch				
C					c				
Y					y				
L					l				
Q					q				
M					m				
Ñ					ñ				
D					d				
N					n				
S					s				
X					x				
I					i				
					a				
E					e				
G					g				
R					r				
V					v				
T					t				
W					w				
					rr				
					g				
				Totales					

Confusiones:

Letras desconocidas:

Comentarios:

Anotaciones:

A   **Respuesta con nombre alfabética:**
anote con ✓

S   **Respuesta con sonido de la letra:**
anote con ✓

Respuesta con sonido de sílaba:
anote con la sílaba

Palabra   Anote la palabra que dice el/la niño/a

Respuesta en inglés:
Anote la respuesta con la letra 'E' (English)

RI   **Respuesta incorrecta:**
Anote lo que dice el/la niño/a.

that works (not necessarily by letter-sound relationships). The child's range of known letters can be expanded by allowing any distinction that works for that child. As more and more letters are controlled, he/she becomes ready for systematic associations like alphabetical names and sound equivalents. *When he/she knows more he/she is more able to be flexible and consider alternatives.*

As it is possible for young children to completely master the particular set of letters in a language, one would expect a child to move gradually over time through the stanine score range until he/she reached perfect scoring for the symbols of the alphabet. An individual child's stanine score indicates his status relative to all children in the age group. It is most useful to contrast a particular child's scores at two points of time to reflect progress.

It is important to note that in Spanish the task titled Identificación de Letras *(Letter Identification)* has produced scores that are very sensitive to instructional procedures. In early Spanish literacy instruction, often the sounds letters make are stressed over the names of the letters. As a result, it is likely that children's responses will reflect a greater awareness of sounds of letters than letter names. Further, depending on the instructional method or program, whole sets of letters may be learned earlier than others. As an example, the *método fónetico* and *método sílabico* are widely used methods to teach Spanish reading. In these programs, the five vowels in Spanish are first taught to students followed by the conso-

nants *m*, *p*, *s*, and *t*. Students learning to read in programs using either of these two methods are likely to know the above letters before they know others.

CONCEPTOS DEL TEXTO IMPRESO *(CONCEPTS ABOUT PRINT)*

The purpose of this task is to obtain an indication about one group of behaviors (control of concepts about print) that support reading acquisition. A check (five to ten minutes) should be made on what children have learned about the way we print languages. Some of the important and easily tested concepts are: the location of the front part of the book, the print (not the picture) tells the story, that there are letters and clusters of letters called words, that there are first letters and last letters in words, that you can choose upper or lower case letters, that spaces are there for a reason, and that different punctuation marks have meanings (fullstop, question mark, talking marks).

Even though we may have tried to explain some of these things we cannot assume that our verbal explanations have taught these children to use their eyes to locate, recognize, and use this information. Concepts about print are learned gradually as the child reads and writes over the first two years of formal schooling.

The booklets required for the Conceptos Del Texto Impreso *(Concepts About Print)* observation are titled

Research Group	Identificación de Letras *(Letter Identification)*									
	Normalized scores—Stanine Groups									
	Stanine Group	**1**	**2**	**3**	**4**	**5**	**6**	**7**	**8**	**9**
Urban Children in first grade in 1991–92 from Arizona, Texas, and Illinois	**Fall 1991 N = 282**	0–6	7–11	12–18	19–26	27–40	41–49	50–54	55–58	59–61
	Mid-Year	0–17	18–32	33–41	42–50	51–56	57	58	59–60	61
	Spring 1992 N = 202	3–19	20–33	34–43	44–52	53–57	58–59	60	61	61

Validity: Correlation with Aprenda Spanish Reading Achievement Test for 282 children in fall 1991; r = .60 Correlation with Aprenda Spanish Reading Achievement Test for 202 children in spring 1992; r = .66 (Escamilla 1992)

Reliability: 282 children in fall 1991, r = .94 ; Cronbach's Alpha Analysis 202 children in spring 1992, r = .96; (Escamilla 1992)

Note: In order to determine a midyear scoring range, the fall and spring scores on each observation task were averaged in the following manner: $\dfrac{Score\ F\ +\ Score\ S}{2}$

Las piedras (Stones) and *Arena (Sand)*. Both are conceptual reconstructions of Clay's booklets. Both can be used with the new entrant to school or the "nonreader" because the child is asked to help the examiner by pointing to certain features as the examiner reads the book. Five-year-old children have some fun, and experience little difficulty with the test items. The test reflects changes in reading skills during the first year of instruction but is of less significance in the subsequent years for the children who make average progress. For problem readers, confusions about these arbitrary conventions of our written language code tend to persist. Conceptos Del Texto Impreso has proved to be a sensitive indicator of one group of behaviors that support reading acquisition. As nonreaders become readers, changes occur in Conceptos Del Texto Impreso scores. This set of observations is able to capture changes over time in the first years of school. Conceptos Del Texto Impreso has been translated and used with Danish- as well as Spanish-speaking children. Unfortunately, the interest in Concepts About Print has resulted in its being lifted from its position as one of a battery of observation tasks in a wide ranging survey designed to monitor changes in a complex set of reading behaviors and expected to stand alone as some indictor of "readiness" or reading progress. It should not be reduced to a mere prediction device when it can be used as a valuable guide for teachers during the early stages of reading acquisition. Important though this learning is, it addresses only one of several areas of necessary learning.

Some important discussions of the original development of the Concepts About Print observation task will be found in Clay (1989, 1991, 1993) and Johns (1980).

Administration

The tasks present a standard situation within which the child can be observed. Try to be flexible enough to communicate the task to the child.

Administer the items according to the instructions given. If the child fails Item 10, then Items 12, 13, and 14 are likely to be failed and can be omitted at the discretion of the examiner. If Items 12, 13, and 14 are omitted, you should still read the story on those pages to the child. Items 15 to 25 should be administered to all children.

Use the instructions for the administration and scoring of this test given on pages 74–77. Use the scoring sheet on page 80.

Before starting, thoroughly familiarize yourself with this test. Use the exact wording given below in each

Otro día
busqué aquel hoyo
Todo lo que vi fue
arena plana, arena suave,
arena como sal, las olas
y arena mojada.
¡Pero ay, ya no está el hoyo!

18

from *Arena*

y la pateé muy fuerte.
Hice mi pie para atrás

10

from *Las piedras*

demonstration. (Read the instructions from the printed text for each administration.)

In Spanish, because of regional varieties and dialects, some words may need to be clarified for children. For example, on Item 12 the word *cerca* (fence) may need to be clarified if a child looks puzzled or questions it. This is because there are many ways to say the word fence in Spanish (e.g., *cerco*). It is important to try to retain a standard task but be flexible enough to communicate the task to the child. If changes in wording are needed to accommodate regional variations, please note the prompt that was effective.

In order to make administration and scoring of this task clear both to bilingual and non-bilingual persons who may be reading this book, the task that each item tests is printed in bold letters in Spanish followed by English italics. Further, what the teacher does as s/he administers the task is also printed in bold letters in Spanish in parentheses followed by English italics—also in parentheses. Finally, what teachers say to children as they administer the task begins with a *guión* (dash) and is also printed in bold letters in Spanish followed by the English italics. Scoring guidelines are printed in English.

Start the task by saying to the child:

Te voy a leer este cuento, pero quiero que me ayudes.

I'm going to read you this story but I want you to help me.

LA CUBIERTA *(COVER)*

Prueba *(Test)* **Orientación del libro. Pase el libro al niño sosteniéndolo verticalmente y con la parte posterior del libro.**
(For orientation of book. Pass the booklet to the child, holding the book vertically by the outside edge, spine toward the child).

Item 1 **Diga** *(Say):* **-Enséñame la parte de enfrente del libro.** *Show me the front of this book.*

Scoring: Score 1 point for the correct response.

PAGINAS 2/3 *(PAGES 2/3)*

Prueba *(Test)* **El texto impreso lleva el sentido y no la ilustración**
(Concept that print, not picture carries the message)

Item 2 **Diga** *(Say):* **-Voy a leer el cuento. Ayúdame. Enséñame dónde empezar a leer.**
-¿Dónde empiezo?
(Lea el texto para el estudiante.)
I'll read this story. You help me. Show me where to start reading. Where do I begin to read? (Read text to child).

Scoring: Score 1 for print. 0 for picture.

PAGINAS 4/5 *(PAGES 4/5)*

Prueba *(Test)* **Las reglas direcciónales**
(For directional rules)

Item 3 **Diga** *(Say):* **-Enséñame dónde empezar.**
Show me where to start.

Scoring: Score 1 for top left.

Item 4 **Diga** *(Say):* **-¿Por dónde sigo?**
Which way do I go?

Scoring: Score 1 for left to right.

Item 5 **Diga** *(Say):* **-¿Y luego a dónde me voy?**
Where do I go after that?

Scoring: Score 1 for return sweep to left.

(Score items 3–5 if all movements are demonstrated in one response.)

Prueba *(Test)* **Aparear palabra por palabra**
(Word-by-word pointing)

Item 6 **Diga** *(Say):* **-Apunta con el dedo mientra leo.**
(Lea despacio pero fluida mente).
Point to it while I read it.
(Read slowly, but fluently.)

Scoring: Score 1 for exact matching.

PAGINA 6 *(PAGE 6)*

Prueba *(Test)* **Concepto del comienzo y el fín**
(Concept of first and last)

Lea el texto al niño.
(Read the text to the child).

Item 7 **Diga** *(Say):* **-Enséñame la primera parte de cuento.**
Show me the first part of the story
-Enséñame la última parte.
Show me the last part.

Scoring: Score 1 point if BOTH are correc in any sense (e.g., applied to th whole text OR to a line, OR to word, OR to a letter).

PAGINA 7 *(PAGE 7)*

Prueba *(Test)* **Inversión del dibujo**
(Inversion of picture)

Item 8 **Diga** *(Say):* **-Enséñame la parte de abajo de dibujo (despacio y con preci sión).**
Show me the bottom of the pictur (slowly and deliberately).
(No mencione que el dibujo est al revés.)
(Do NOT mention upside-down.)

Scoring: Score 1 for verbal explanation OR for pointing to the top of the page OR for turning the book around and pointing appropriately.

PAGINAS 8/9 (PAGES 8/9)

Prueba *(Test)* **Respuesta al texto impreso invertido**
Response to inverted print

Item 9   Diga *(Say):* **-¿Dónde empiezo?**
Where do I begin?
-¿Por dónde sigo?
Which way do I go?
-¿Y luego a dónde me voy después?
Where do I go after that?
(Ahora lea el texto para el estudiante.)
(Read the text to the child.)

Scoring: Score 1 for beginning with **"La"** *(Las piedras)* and **"Las"** *(Arena)* moving right to left across the lower and then the upper line. OR 1 for turning the book around and moving left to right in the conventional manner.

PAGINAS 10/11 (PAGES 10/11)

Prueba *(Test)* **Cambio del orden de las líneas**
(Line Sequence)

Item 10   Diga *(Say):* **-¿Qué tiene de mal esta parte? (Lea inmediatamente la línea de abajo y despúes la línea de arriba.) (NO apunte hacia el texto.)**
What's wrong with this?
(Read immediately the bottom line first, then the top line. Do NOT point.)

Scoring: Score 1 for comment on line order.

PAGINAS 12/13 (PAGES 12/13)

Prueba *(Test)* **Página del lado izquierdo antes de la derecha.**

(A left page is read before a right page.)

Item 11   Diga *(Say):* **-¿Dónde empiezo a leer?**
Where do I start reading?

Scoring: Score 1 point for left page indication.

Prueba *(Test)* **Un cambio del orden de las palabras**
(Word sequence)

Item 12   Diga *(Say):* **-¿Qué tiene de mal esta página? (Señale la página 12, NO al texto. Lea el texto despacio como si estuviera escrito correcto.)**
(What's wrong with this page?)
(Point to the page number 12, NOT the text. Read the text slowly as if it were correct.)

Scoring: Score 1 point for comment on either error.

Prueba *(Test)* **Un cambio del orden de las letras**
(Letter order)

Item 13   Diga *(Say):* **-¿Qué tiene de mal esta página? (Señale la página 13, NO al texto. Lea el texto despacio como si estuviera escrito correcto.)**
(What's wrong on this page? Point to the page number 13, NOT the text. Read slowly as if it were correct.)

Scoring: Score 1 point for any ONE reordering of letters that is noticed and explained.

PAGINAS 14/15 (PAGES 14/15)

Prueba *(Test)* **Un cambio del orden le las letras dentro de una palabra.**
(Reordering of letters within a word)

Item 14   Diga *(Say):* **-¿Qúe tiene de mal la escritura de esta página? (Lea el texto despacio como si estuviera escrito correcto.)**
What's wrong with the writing on

this page? (Read the text slowly as if it were correct.)

Scoring: Score 1 point for ONE error noticed.

Prueba (Test) **Significado de los signos de interrogación**
(Meaning of a question mark)

Item 15 Diga (Say): **-¿Para qué son estos?**
What's this for?
(Apunte o trace con un lápiz o el dedo los signos de interrogación.)
What's this for?
(Point to or trace the question mark with a finger or pencil.)

Scoring: Score 1 point for explanation of function or name.

PAGINAS 16/17 (PAGES 16/17)

Prueba (Test) **Significado de los signos de puntuación**
(Punctuation)
(Lea el texto.) *(Read the text.)*

Diga (Say): **-¿Para qué con estos?**
What's this for?

Item 16 **(Apunte o trace con un lápiz el signo del punto.)**
(Point to or trace with a pencil the period.)

Item 17 **(Apunte o trace con un lápiz el signo de la coma.)**
(Point to or trace with a pencil the comma.)

Item 18 **(Apunte o trace con un lápiz los guiónes.)**
(Point to or trace with a pencil the quotation marks.)

Item 19 **(Apunte o trace con un lápiz el acento.)**
(Point to or trace with a pencil the accent mark.)

Scoring: Score 1 point each for explanation of function or name.

Prueba (Test) **La correspondencia entre letras mayúsculas y letras minúsculas**
(Capital and lower-case correspondence)

Item 20 Diga (Say): **-Busca una letra minúscula (chiquita) como esta.**
Las piedras o Arena: Apunta la letra A (mayúscula), y demuestra (apuntando) a la letra A mayúscula y la letra a minúscula si el niño no lo sabe hacer.
(Point to capital A and demonstrate by pointing to an upper case A and a lower case a if the child does not succeed.)

Las piedras: Señale las letras mayúsculas *P*, *E*.

Arena: Señale las letras mayūsculas *E*, *M*.

Scoring: *Las piedras:* Score 1 point if BOTH *Pp* and *Ee* are located.
Arena: Score 1 point if BOTH *Ee* and *Mm* are located.

PAGINAS 18/19 *(PAGES 18/19)*

Prueba (Test) **Palabras Reversibles** *(Reversible Words)*

Item 21 *Las piedras* **(Lea el texto.)**

Diga (Say): **-Enséñame la palabra *la*.**
Show me the word la.
-Enséñame la palabra *ya*.
Show me the word ya.

Arena **(Lea el texto.)**

Diga (Say): **-Enséñame la palabra *ya*.**
Show me the word ya.
-Enséñame la palabra *las*.
Show me the word las.

Scoring: Score 1 point for BOTH correct.

PAGINA 20 *(PAGE 20)*

Prueba (Test) **Conceptos de Letras** *(Letter Concepts)*

Have two pieces of light card (13 × 5 cm) that the child can hold and slide easily over the line of text to block out words and letters. To start lay the cards on the page but leave all print exposed. Open the cards out between each question asked.

Item 22 **Diga** *(Say):* -Este cuento *(Las piedras)* dice: "La piedra rodó para abajo de la loma." [o *(Arena)* "Las olas salpicaron dentro el hoyo."]
-Mueva la tarjetas encima de la línea así, hasta que se vea solamente una letra; dos letras. (Demuestre el movimiento de las tarjetas pero no haga el ejercicio.)
This story (Stones) *says—"The stone rolled down the hill." [or* (Sand) *"The waves splashed in the hole."] I want you to push the cards across the story like this until all you can see is (deliberately with stress) just one letter. (Demonstrate the movement of the cards but do not do the exercise.)*

Diga *(Say):* -Enséñame dos letras.
Show me two letters.

Scoring: Score 1 point for BOTH correct.

Prueba *(Test)* **Concepto de palabras** *(Word concept)*

Item 23 **Diga** *(Say):* -Enséñame una palabra.
Show me just one word.
Ahora, enséñame dos palabras.
Now show me two words.

Scoring: Score 1 point for BOTH correct.

Prueba *(Test)* **Conceptos de la primera y la última letra**
(First and last letter concepts)

Item 24 **Diga** *(Say):* -Enséñame la primera letra de una palabra.
Show me the first letter of a word.
-Enséñame la última letra de una palabra.
Show me the last letter of a word.

Scoring: 1 point for BOTH correct.

Prueba *(Test)* **Concepto de letra mayúscula**
(Capital letter concepts)

Item 25 **Diga** *(Say):* -Enséñame una letra mayúscula.
Show me a capital letter.

Scoring: Score 1 point if correct.

Scoring

Score items as instructed on pages 74–77. In addition, if a child answers in English, record English responses with a check mark and "E." English responses are counted as correct if they are used instead of an equivalent Spanish word. As an example, a child may say *period* instead of *punto*. This is a correct response and should be recorded as noted above. Use the table below to convert these scores to a stanine score.

Interpretation of scores

The Conceptos del Texto Impreso *(Concepts About Print)* measured in this observation task are a limited set of information that can be learned in the first years of school. For this reason, young children will test low early in their schooling, and their stanine scores should increase as their reading improves. The test's greatest value is diagnostic. Items should uncover concepts to be learned or confusions to be untangled. For teaching purposes, examine the child's performance and teach the unknown concepts. The items are not in a strict difficulty sequence. Again, the age at which children pass each item will be very dependent on the teaching program and method-emphasis used in a particular school.

Most of these Conceptos del Texto Impreso items tell us something about what the child is attending to on the printed page. The items in which the order of the letters or words has been changed are particularly sensitive to shifts in children's visual attention to detail in print. It is not immediately obvious to teachers who use Conceptos del Texto Impreso that there is a steep gradient of difficulty in items 12 to 14. Children usually notice the changed word order (12) before a change in first and last letters (13) or a change in the middle letters (14) buried within the word.

PRUEBA DE PALABRAS *(WORD TEST)*

Standardized word tests are based on the principle of sampling from the child's reading vocabulary. They are meant to sample high frequency words the child may have had the opportunity to learn. They cannot be reliable

Research Group	Conceptos del Texto Impreso *(Concepts About Print)*									
	Normalized Scores—Stanine Groups									
	Stanine Group	1	2	3	4	5	6	7	8	9
Urban Children in first grade in 1991–92 from Arizona, Texas, and Illinois	**Fall 1991 N = 282**	0–3	4–6	7–8	9	10–11	12–13	14–15	16–17	18–21
	Mid-Year	0–4	5–8	9	10–12	13–14	15	16–17	18–19	20–21
	Spring 1992 N = 202	5–6	7–9	10–11	12–13	14–15	16–17	18–19	20–21	22–23

Validity: *Correlation with Aprenda Spanish Reading Achievement Test for 282 children in fall 1991; r = .53. Correlation with Aprenda Spanish Reading Achievement Test for 202 children in spring 1992; r = .51 (Escamilla 1992)*

Reliability: *282 children in fall 1991, r = .69; Cronbach's Alpha Analysis 202 children in spring 1992, r = .82; (Escamilla 1992)*

Note: *In order to determine a midyear scoring range, the fall and spring scores on each observation task were averaged in the following manner:* $\dfrac{Score\ F\ +\ Score\ S}{2}$

until the child has acquired sufficient vocabulary to make sampling a feasible measurement strategy.

For early identification a different approach is required. Word lists can be compiled from the high frequency words in the reading materials that are adopted. The principle here is a sampling from the high frequency words of that restricted corpus from which the child has had the opportunity to learn. The following test was devised for Spanish-speaking children who were using various Spanish language basal readers in 1989 in Tucson, Arizona. Using *the Cornejo Spanish Word Frequency List* (1980), the *Santillana Basal Spanish Reading Program* (1984), and the *Brigance Spanish Word Frequency List* (1984), lists of frequently occurring words were constructed. Three hundred first grade children were then asked to read these words and a statistical tool known as a P-value was utilized to calculate and compare the most difficult and least difficult words for these children. These P-values were calculated for the fall and for the spring for the first grade children in the study (Escamilla 1992). From results of this study, it was determined that each of the three word lists included words that had a range of difficulty. The three sources of frequently used words cited above contain reading vocabulary words which the young Spanish-speaking learner has most likely already been exposed to.

It should be noted that any test of first year instruction must be closely linked to that instruction. The *most frequently occurring words* in whatever children's literature or basic reading texts being used will probably provide a satisfactory source of test items.

Administration
Prueba de Palabras *(Word Test)* takes about two minutes to administer. The test sheet (p. 82) can be copied and mounted on a clipboard for easy administration.

Ask a child to read *one* list. Give Lista A *(List A)* or Lista B *(List B)* or Lista C *(List C)*. Help the child with the practice word if necessary and never score it. Do not help with any other words and do not use the list for teaching. Use alternative lists for retesting.

Use of the test
The score will indicate the extent to which a child is accumulating a reading vocabulary of some of the most frequently used words included in Spanish reading materials. These scores may be used, together with teachers' observations recorded for book reading, for grouping and regrouping children. Successive tests will indicate whether a progressive change is occurring in the child's reading performance.

Una Guía De Estándares Para Los Resultados

1 La parte de enfrente del libro.

2 Texto impreso (no una ilustración).

3 Apunta hacia arriba, a la izquierda, 'Tomé' ... (Arena); 'Vi un' ... (Las piedras)

4 Mueve el dedo de izquierda a derecha en cualquier línea.

5 Mueve el dedo de la punta del lado derecho de una línea más arriba a la otra punta del lado izquierdo, de la siguiente línea abajo, o lo mueve hacia abajo de la página.

6 Aparear las palabras con el dedo.

7 Ambos conceptos deben estar correctos, pero se puede mostrar en todo el texto completo o en una sola línea, palabra o letra.

8 Explicación oral se demuestra con apuntar hacia arriba de la página.

9 Se da crédito si empieza con la palabra 'Las' (Arena) o con 'La' (Las piedras) y se mueve de la derecha a izquierda a través de la línea más abajo y después en la línea de arriba, o volteando el libro y moviendo de la izquierda a la derecha en una manera convencional de movimiento.

10 Dar una explicación que implique que el orden de la línea ha sido cambiado.

11 Dice o muestra que la página del lado izquierdo precede la página del lado derecho.

12 Se fija, por lo menos, en un cambio en el orden de las palabras.

13 Se fija, por lo menos, en un cambio en el orden de las letras.

14 Se fija, por lo menos, en un cambio en el orden de las letras.

15 Dice 'Punto de interrogación', o 'Una pregunta', o 'Pregunta algo'.

16 Dice 'Parar', 'Punto', o 'Punto final;' 'Cuando no hay más' o 'Es el fin'.

17 Dice 'Paras un poquito' o 'Para descansar' o 'Una coma'.

18 Dice 'Cuando alguien está hablando', 'Para hablar', 'Es un guión'.

19 Dice: 'Acento',o 'La palabra es diferente (no es igual)' o dan un ejemplo (mamá; papá; un nombre - López).

20 Señala dos pares de mayúsculas y minúsculas.

21 Apunta correctamente a las dos palabras, 'la' y 'ya' (Las piedras) 'las' y 'ya' (Arena)

22 Identifica una y dos letras a petición.

23 Identifica una y dos palabras a petición.

24 Identifica una primera y una última letra.

25 Identifica una letra mayúscula.

RESULTADOS DE LOS CONCEPTOS
DEL TEXTO IMPRESO

Fecha _____

Nombre _____ Edad _____ RESULTADO [   ]

Observador _____ Fecha de Nacimiento _____ GRUPO ESTANINA [   ]

PÁGINA	RESULTADO	PREGUNTA	COMENTARIO
La cubierta		1. Parte de adelante	
2/3		2. El texto impreso lleva el mensaje (no la ilustración)	
4/5 4/5 4/5 4/5		3. Dónde empezar 4. Dónde seguir 5. Regresar a la izquierda 6. Aparear palabra por palabra	
6		7. Concepto de principio y fin	
7		8. La parte de abajo del dibujo	
8/9		9. Empezar en el renglón de abajo con "La" *(Las piedras)* o "Las" *(La arena)*, y luego pasar al renglón de arriba o voltear el libro	
10/11		10. Cambio del orden de los renglones	
12/13 12/13 12/13		11. Página izquierda antes que la derecha 12. Un cambio en el orden de las palabras 13. Un cambio en el orden de las letras	
14/15 14/15		14. Un cambio en el orden de las letras 15. Significado de ¿?	
16/17 16/17 16/17 16/17		16. Significado del punto 17. Significado de la coma 18. Significado de la raya *(Las piedras)* Significado de las comillas *(Arena)* 19. Significado de la tilde (acento ortográfico) 20. Encuentra P p, E e *(Las piedras)* o E e M m *(Arena)*	
18/19		21. Palabras reversibles: "la", "ya" *(Las piedras)*; "las", "ya" *(Arena)*	
20 20 20 20		22. Una letra; dos letras 23. Una palabra; dos palabras 24. Primera y última letra de una palabra 25. Letra mayúscula	

Scoring

The table below shows scores on the Prueba de Palabras (*Word Test*) for a large sample of children in the first grade in the fall of 1991 and again in the spring of 1992. Stanines distribute scores according to the normal curve in groups from 1, the lowest, to 9. It is possible for children to completely master this learning. One would therefore expect a child to move through the stanine score range until s/he reached perfect scoring.

On this task, as on others, responses in English are counted as correct. For example, the words *me, come,* and *no* are words that can be read either in Spanish or English and make sense.

What the test does not do

- It does not give a reading age.
- It does not discriminate between better readers after one year of instruction. On the contrary, it groups them together.
- Differences of less than three score points are not sufficiently reliable to support any decisions about the child's progress without other evidence.
- It does not sample a child's reading performance if s/he is working beyond the level of the early reading materials used to derive this test.

ESCRITURA DE VOCABULARIO (*WRITING VOCABULARY*)

Examine examples of the child's writing behavior. Does s/he have good letter formation? How many letter forms does s/he have? Does s/he have a small repertoire of words s/he can construct from memory with the letters correctly sequenced? What are they?

By observing children as they write we can learn a great deal about what they understand about print and messages in print and what features of print they are attending to. Writing behavior is a good indicator of a child's knowledge of letters and of the left-to-right sequencing behavior required to read both Spanish and English. In writing words letter-by-letter the child must recall not only the configuration but also the details of letter formation and letter order. A child's written texts are a good source of information about his visual discrimination of print, for as the child learns to write words, the hand and the eye support and supplement each other to organize the learner's first attempts to discover how to distinguish different letters one from another (a large set of visual discrimination learning).

Research Group	Prueba de Palabras (*Word Test*) Normalized Scores—Stanine Groups									
	Stanine Group	1	2	3	4	5	6	7	8	9
Urban Children in first grade in 1991–92 from Arizona, Texas, and Illinois	**Fall 1991 N = 282**	0	0	0	0	0–2	3–5	6–12	13–17	18–20
	Mid-Year	0	0	1	2–8	9–15	16–18	19	20	20
	Spring 1992 N = 202	0	0	1–2	3–10	11–18	19	20	20	20

Validity: Correlation with Aprenda Spanish Reading Achievement Test for 282 children in fall 1991; r = .72 Correlation with Aprenda Spanish Reading Achievement Test for 202 children in spring 1992; r = .75 (Escamilla 1992)

Reliability: 282 children in fall 1991, r = .95; Cronbach's Alpha Analysis 202 children in spring 1992, r = .97; (Escamilla 1992)

Note: In order to determine a midyear scoring range, the fall and spring scores on each observation task were averaged in the following manner: $\dfrac{Score\ F\ +\ Score\ S}{2}$

Lista A	Lista B	Lista C
Palabra de Práctica con	Palabra de Práctica en	Palabra de Práctica veo
yo	mira	hace
pero	y	vamos
son	el	come
aquí	tiene	las
abajo	como	muy
mi	la	jugar
es	dijo	tu
soy	corre	para
donde	por	fue
feliz	voy	tengo
también	está	cada
da	grande	quiero
una	puedo	ella
me	no	al
bonito	alto	todo
toma	que	este
casa	más	rojo
sí	busca	de
gusta	del	lee
de	un	se

RESULTADOS DE LA PRUEBA DE PALABRA
Use una de las siguientes listas

Fecha _____

Nombre _____ Edad _____ RESULTADO [/ 20]

Observador _____ Fecha de Nacimiento _____ GRUPO ESTANINA [ ]

Registre las respuestas incorrectas al lado de la palabra.

LISTA A	LISTA B	LISTA C
yo	mira	hace
pero	y	vamos
son	el	come
aquí	tiene	las
abajo	como	muy
mi	la	jugar
es	dijo	tu
soy	corre	para
donde	por	fue
feliz	voy	tengo
también	está	cada
da	grande	quiero
una	puedo	ella
me	no	al
bonito	alto	todo
toma	que	este
casa	más	rojo
sí	busca	de
gusta	del	lee
de	un	se

COMENTARIO:

Writing samples

Rating techniques can be used on children's early attempts to write stories. For example, to rate writing in the first year of school take three samples of the child's stories on consecutive days or for three successive weeks and rate them as follows for language level, message quality, and directional features. (One sample is not sufficiently reliable for this evaluation technique.)

Language level
Record the number of the highest level of linguistic organization used by the child.

1 Alphabetical (letters)
2 Word (any recognizable word)
3 Word group (any two-word phrase)
4 Sentence (any simple sentence)
5 Punctuated story (of two or more sentences)
6 Paragraphed story (two themes)

Message quality
Record the number for the best description of the child's sample.

1 S/he has a concept of signs (uses letters, invents letters, uses punctuation).
2 S/he has a concept that a message is conveyed.
3 S/he copied a message.
4 S/he makes repetitive use of sentence patterns such as "Here is a . . . ." "Este/esta es una . . . ."
5 S/he attempts to record own ideas.
6 S/he completed a successful composition.

Directional principles
Record the number of the highest rating for which there is no error in the sample of the child's writing.

1 S/he shows no evidence of directional knowledge
2 S/he shows knowledge of part of the directional pattern: start top left, *or* move left to right, *or* return down left
3 S/he shows reversal of the directional pattern (right to left and return down right)
4 S/he uses correct directional pattern
5 S/he correct directional pattern and spaces between words
6 S/he writes extensive text without any difficulties of arrangement and spacing

RATING WRITING SAMPLES

	A LANGUAGE LEVEL	**B** MESSAGE QUALITY	**C** DIRECTIONAL PRINCIPLES
Not yet satisfactory	1–4	1–4	1–4
Probably satisfactory	5–6	5–6	5–6

Sometimes what children learn falls outside the limits of the analysis categories teachers use. Michael was five and in his first year of school, but at home he had access to his father's computer. Unaided he "pecked out" this story on the keyboard bypassing the need to form letters.

> *Mr. snowe by michael.
> wun cod and snowee morning a boy came out to plae and he made a snoe man and when it wa nite time farethe cris mis came to visit adlaide.

The story combines local knowledge (of Adelaide, Australia) with the story knowledge about "snowee" mornings and snowmen that do not occur in Adelaide and with fantasy knowledge about "farethe cris mis."

A similar phenomenon was observed with Alex in Spanish. Alex was at the end of his first grade year when he created the following story and wrote it on a computer during computer time at his school. Again, his ability to do this kind of story on the computer bypasses his need to form letters.

> El dia en que me hice un ratonsito.
> Yo me fui de mi casa y arepente me ise un ratonsito y despues mire un queso y lo agarre y me lo comi y me querian matar y me meti en un oyito de la casa. y despues segi comiendo y comiendo.

> *The day I became a mouse.*
> *I went out of my house and all of a sudden I became a mouse and*
> *then I saw a piece of cheese and I grabbed it and I ate it*
> *and they wanted to kill me and I went into a hole of a house and them I continued to eat and eat.*

(*Taken from: Clay, M. M. 1993. *An Observation Survey of Early Literacy Achievement.* Portsmouth, NH: Heinemann.)

Alex's story relates his knowledge of mice and how he might act if he suddenly became a mouse. His use of invented spelling that is phonetically appropriate demonstrates he has a great deal of knowledge of sound/symbol correspondence in Spanish. Further, his story has a logical sequence and a plot.

It is part of the fun of making careful observations of children who are writing that we can reflect on how they draw from diverse sources of knowledge as they construct their stories.

ESCRITURA DE VOCABULARIO (WRITING VOCABULARY)

Clay's *English Observation Survey* (1993) was based on more than twenty-seven years of research. One of these studies involved observing the writing of one hundred children once every week (Clay 1966). A result of this study was the realization that competent children made lists of all the words they knew. These lists of words were very interesting. A sample of one child's word list is included.

Examine Mark's list, produced spontaneously at home when he was five years and eleven months old. Assuming that he was writing down the page, notice how a word he has just written seems to suggest another word he might write. Mark found words that started the same (*It, is, in*), that ended the same (*at, bat, hat*), that were opposites (*come, go*), that form a category of family names (*Mum, Dad, Mark, Denise*), that are the same but different (*car, cat, bell, ball*), and so on.

From this study, one of Clay's research students, Susan E. Robinson (1973) devised a useful observation task that has all the properties of a good test when it is used in the first two years of school. Robinson's writing vocabulary task is like a screen upon which the child can project what he/she knows—not only what we have taught him/her but what s/he has learned anywhere in his various worlds. The child samples his/her own universe of knowledge. This is appropriate because when learners are near the beginning of learning in a new field the kind of sampling of knowledge used in test construction does not work—what you are sampling for is in very short supply. At first there is not enough common knowledge among beginners to use such a sampling approach.

A task was constructed in which the child was encouraged to write down all the words he/she knew how to write, starting with his/her own name and making a personal list of words he/she had managed to learn. This simple test was reliable (i.e., a child tended to score at a similar level when retested within two weeks) and had

Mark's list

a high relationship with reading words in isolation. Even at the kindergarten stage, a child can respond to the instruction "Write all the words you know." How children respond changes over time, and highly competent children can demonstrate long lists of words even after a limited time at school.

Robinson's procedure can be easily applied in Spanish or any other language as only the directions and prompts to the child need to be reconstructed. This is an assessment that a teacher can do in any place, at any time, needing nothing but her personal knowledge of how to make such observations and score them in systematic ways.

Although some children will write nothing or just the

first letter of their name, other children will write more than seventy words in ten minutes, the time allowed for this observation. This provides a score that correlates well with other literacy measures, changes over time, and has good measurement qualities. When the child can write more than seventy words, the value of this score for telling us about change in literacy control diminishes. After that the teacher can begin to measure how the child works with a more traditional spelling or writing task.

When the developers of *El Instrumento de Observación* constructed the Clay and Robinson tasks in Spanish, they found that the task enabled teachers to observe children at work in the same way in Spanish as they had in English. Further, this task in Spanish also had good measurement qualities in that it was highly reliable (reliability in Spanish was established by administering this task to three hundred children one week and then retesting them on the same task one week later). These children tended to score at a similar level when retested (r = .95—fall 1991; r = .87—spring 1992; see Escamilla 1992).

A sample of a writing vocabulary task in Spanish is included below. Notice how this student's sample illustrates that these lists in Spanish are equally as interesting and valuable as those generated in English.

As we examine this student's (Cristina's) writing sample, we will assume that she was writing down the page. Notice how, just as in English, a word she has written seems to suggest another word she might write. Cristina turned singular words into plurals (e.g., *la, las, mi, mis, el, los*); she wrote words that are part of word families in Spanish (e.g., *un, una, uno, unas*); she wrote verb conjugations for some common verbs (e.g., *come, como, comes; va, van, vas*); she wrote names of animals in their masculine and feminine form (e.g., *gato, gata; oso, osa*); and she wrote words that form a category of family names (*mamá, papá, nana*), and so on. The observations of the work of three hundred students on this task along with the results of the validity and reliability studies led us to conclude that the writing vocabulary task in Spanish (*Vocabulario de Escritura*) was a valuable tool in order to obtain an indication of a child's ability to recall and record the configuration and details of words.

As with the English writing vocabulary task and other observation tasks, this one is very useful for a short period of time (about two years), telling us how fast a child is building control over a basic writing vocabulary.

Once formal schooling begins, the distribution of scores on this observation task changes markedly with age. For example, in studies on English writing vocabulary tasks, Robinson (1973) found that the mean score

Cristina's sample

for writing vocabulary for children who were five years and six months old was **6.49** with a standard deviation of **4.64**. Two samples of six-year-old children on the same task yielded a mean score of **26.5** and **30.3** respectively with standard deviations of **15.8** for both samples. These samples indicate a significant difference in writing vocabulary development between the five-year, six-month-old subjects and the six-year-old subjects. Note, they represent an age difference of only six months. This provides evidence of the rapid change children make in writing vocabulary once they begin the process of formal schooling.

A group of three hundred Spanish-speaking children were given this writing vocabulary test at the beginning of first grade (fall 1991), and again in the spring (1992), seven months later. The mean score on the fall writing vocabulary task in Spanish was **10.8** with a standard deviation of **11.4**, and in the spring the mean score was **32.4** with a standard deviation of **19.7**. These results parallel those obtained in English and indicate the rapid growth in Spanish writing vocabulary that also occurs when Spanish-speaking children receive formal reading and writing instruction in Spanish (see Escamilla 1992).

Writing Vocabulary (*Vocabulario de Escritura*) scores are very sensitive to the instructional procedures of the classroom. High scores will be associated with very different programs that (a) foster early writing or (b) place an emphasis on word learning. Low scores will be associated with programs that (a) provide few opportunities for children to write or (b) encourage writing but expect only invented spellings.

In the first year of school there is probably a high degree of interdependence between reading words and writing words, but it should not be assumed that success in the first years of learning to read would be assured simply by teaching children to write words.

Administration
As stated above, the purpose of this task is to obtain an indication of a child's ability to recall and record the configuration and details of words. The child is allowed ten minutes to complete this task (an observation sheet is provided on p. 90). In order to make this task understandable to persons who are bilingual or who may only speak English, the instructions for administration have been written in Spanish in bold letters and are also printed in English in italics. Instructions to the child should only be given in Spanish, although the child may respond in both Spanish and English. A detailed account of how to examine student responses is outlined below.

Start by giving the child a blank piece of paper and a pencil and then say:

Quiero ver cuantas palabras puedes escribir.
(I want to see how many words you can write)

¿Puedes escribir tu nombre?
(Can you write your name?)

(Empiece a contar los diez minutos.)
(Start the ten-minute timing here.)

- **Si el niño/la niña dice "no" pregúntele si sabe escribir palabras de una o dos letras**
If the child says "No" ask him/her if he/she knows any single letter or two-letter words.

Diga *(Say)*:
¿Sabes escribir ¿Y?, ¿el?, ¿o?, ¿mi?, ¿la?
Do you know how to write y, el, o, mi, la?

Y después, sugiera otras palabras que quizás sepa (vea abajo)
Then suggest other words that he/she may know how to write (see below).

- **Si el niño dice "sí" diga: -Escribe tu nombre**
If the child says "yes" say, Write your name.

When the child finishes, say:

Bien, ahora, piensa en todas las palabras que tu sabes escribir y escríbelas.
Good. Now think of all the words you know how to write and write them all down.

Dele hasta diez minutos para escribir las palabras. Si para de escribir o si necesita ayuda diga:
-¿Sabes como escribir *yo* o *a*?
-¿Sabes como escribir *ti* o *mi*?

Give the child up to ten minutes to write the words. When he stops writing, or when he needs prompting, suggest words he/she might know how to write.

- Do you know how to write yo *or* a?
- Do you know how to write ti *or* mi?

Use una lista de palabras que el niño encontraría en sus libros de lectura u otros lugares: *yo, a, es, en, soy, para, mamá, gusta, ve, y, papá, gato, sube, mira, de, la, me, casa, amo, oso, se, veo.*

Go through a list of words that the child might have met in his/her reading books or might be able to work out how to write. For example, yo, a, es, en, soy, para, mamá, gusta, ve, y, papá, gato, sube, mira, de, la, me, casa, amo, oso, se, veo.

Continue for ten minutes or until the child's writing vocabulary is exhausted. Prompt the child as much as you like with words s/he might be able to write. Be careful not to interfere with his/her thinking and his/her searching of his/her own repertoire. Very able children need little prompting, but sometimes it is necessary to suggest a category of words. The following questions suggest some examples.

- **Las siguientes categorías de palabras se pueden usar para motivar al estudiante:**

-¿Sabes cómo escribir nombres de miembros de tu familia?
-¿Sabes cómo escribir nombres de amigos?
-¿Sabes cómo escribir nombres de animales?
-¿Sabes cómo escribir nombres de colores?
-¿Sabes cómo escribir nombres de partes o cuartos de la casa (cocina; sala . . .)?
-¿Sabes cómo escribir nombres de comidas?
-¿Sabes cómo escribir nombres de modos de transportación?

- *You can use the following categories of words to help prompt the student.*

Do you know how to write names of members of your family?

Do you know how to write names of friends?

Do you know how to write names of animals?

Do you know how to write names of colors?

Do you know how to write names of parts or rooms in your house (kitchen, living room . . .)?

Do you know how to write names of foods?

Do you know how to write names of things you ride on—or in?

It is not a requirement of this observation that the child be able to read the words he/she has written.

Scoring

Correct spelling

Each completed word scores one point if it is correctly spelled. Do not count the word as correct:

- if the child accidentally writes a word that is correct but spontaneously tells you that it is another word. For example, s/he writes *am* and says without prompting that it is *on* or in the case of Spanish s/he writes *se* and reads *es*.
- if the observer realizes from something else that the child does that s/he does not know what word s/he has written.
- if the tilde (ñ) in the letter **ñ** is omitted from a word containing that letter.

Accent marks

Omission of an accent mark does not influence the scoring unless the omission of the accent mark changes the meaning of the word.

(examples):	tambien	tia	zoologico
	también	tía	zoológico
			(all correct responses)

In cases where inclusion or omission of an accent mark determines an alternate meaning, the written response is accepted unless a specific word has been prompted by the teacher or has been indicated by the child.

(examples):

T: Escribe *está*	C: writes *esta*	(incorrect response)
C: Yo puedo escribir *mamá*	C: writes *mama*	(incorrect response)
T: (no prompts)	C: writes *papa*	(correct response)

Reversed letters

The formation of individual letters (including the reversal of letters) does not influence the scoring except when the letter form represents a different letter. So words with one or more reversed letters are correct when the intended letters are clear (e.g., *bus* for *bus* in English; *las* for *las* in Spanish), but are not correct if the reversed letter could be a different letter (e.g., *bog* for *dog* in English; *bel* for *del* in Spanish).

Words written right to left

These are scored as correct only if the child actually wrote the letters in reverse order. Individual letters may or may not be reversed which means that words scored as correct may have a mixture of reversed and correctly oriented letters. Spanish examples include:

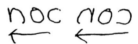

Series of words

Each word is counted in a derived series like *miro, mira, miran* or in a rhyming set or spelling pattern group like *ve, de, me, se;* or *con, pon, son.*

Capital letters

Capital letters are acceptable substitutions for lower-case letters and vice versa.

English words

English and code-switching responses are acceptable when written correctly, and when they meet all the scoring criteria outlined above (e.g., *mom, dad, K-Mart, love*). A code-switching response is one that is written in one language but prompted or read in another. For example, the teacher prompts, "¿Sabes escribir mamá?" *(Do you know how to write mamá?)* The child says "sí" and then writes "mom." In these cases, the child who is code-switching may be relating the prompt *mamá* to the most visual experience, which may be *mom* as written in English. In this case, *mom* in English fits with the child's concept of the written word *mamá*. These responses are counted as correct and should be noted.

Interpreting the observation

From the Escamilla study reported above, you should note that the mean score for first grade Spanish-speaking students on the writing task in the fall of their first grade year was **10.8**. That means that the majority of students in the study could not write more than ten words. The results for children in the spring of their first grade year were far

Research Group	Escritura de Vocabulario *(Writing Vocabulary)* Normalized Scores—Stanine Groups									
	Stanine Group	1	2	3	4	5	6	7	8	9
Urban Children in first grade in 1991–92 from Arizona, Texas, and Illinois	**Fall 1991 N = 282**	0	1	2	3–4	5–7	8–15	16–23	24–33	34–71
	Mid-Year	0–1	2–4	5–13	14–25	26–39	40–50	51–57	58–69	70–80
	Spring 1992 N = 202	0–2	3–5	6–15	16–27	28–41	42–52	53–59	60–71	72–82

Validity: *Correlation with Aprenda Spanish Reading Achievement Test for 282 children in fall 1991; r = .66 Correlation with Aprenda Spanish Reading Achievement Test for 202 children in spring 1992; r = .65 (Escamilla 1992)*

Reliability: *282 children in fall 1991, r = .95; Test/Retest 202 children in spring 1992, r = .87; Test/Retest (Escamilla 1992)*

Note: *In order to determine a midyear scoring range, the fall and spring scores on each observation task were averaged in the following manner:* $\dfrac{Score\ F\ +\ Score\ S}{2}$

higher, the mean score being **32.4**. Even with the ten-minute limit, the writing vocabulary of able children was by no means exhausted. Some children wrote more than seventy words in ten minutes. There are marked individual differences among children in the first year of school.

A poor writing vocabulary may indicate that, despite all her/his efforts to read, a child is in fact taking very little notice of the visual differences in print. S/he requires an all-out teaching effort and a great deal of help to elicit early writing behaviors. In this learning, the hand and eye support and supplement each other. Only later does the eye become the solo agent and learning becomes faster than in the eye-plus-hand learning stage (Clay 1991).

Many kinds of experiences, in school and out of school, with letters, numbers, words, stories, drawing, and life in the real world have enabled the child to learn such things about print as where it is used and what kinds of things it can tell us. Despite a high degree of interdependence between reading and writing words, they are not necessarily linked, according to the studies of spellers. Some children cannot read words that they can write, and vice versa. Further, instructional programs vary in the extent to which they allow or foster this reciprocity.

Keeping records of progress

A record of a child's progress may be kept in one of the following ways:

An inventory of writing vocabulary

If the writing observation is done at several points of time—at entry, after six months, and after one year, this provides one type of record of change over time in early writing. In the example on page 92, the progress of another child called Beatriz is clear from the record itself without any reference to scores or stanines.

A record of change over time in daily or weekly writing

A teacher can keep a list of new words written independently by certain students to whom she is currently paying particular attention (see Writing Vocabulary Weekly Record Sheet, p. 91).

A graph of writing progress

The teacher could make a graph of these accumulated totals. To start the record for Week I, s/he enters the number of words written correctly on the initial writing vocabulary observation task. Each week the teacher adds, cumulatively, the number of new words the child wrote independently in the stories s/he was writing in the classroom. The cumulative record of writing vocabulary is a sensitive reflection of the child's increasing control over writing, and it is a reliable indicator of slow progress.

OBSERVACIÓN DE LA ESCRITURA DE VOCABULARIO

Resultado

Fecha: _____

Nombre: _____ Escuela: _____ Grado: _____

Maestra/o de clase: _____ Observador: _____

Doble el encabezado hacia atrás antes de que el niño/la niña use la hoja.

COMENTARIO:

REGISTRO SEMANAL DE LA ESCRITURA DE VOCABULARIO

Nombre: _____

Fecha de Nacimiento: _____

Prueba Inicial: Fecha:	Semana: Fecha:	Semana: Fecha:	Semana: Fecha:	Semana: Fecha:
Semana: Fecha:	Semana: Fecha:	Semana: Fecha:	Semana: Fecha:	Semana: Fecha:

Fall 1991

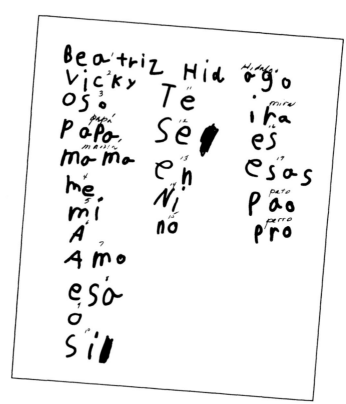

Spring 1992

Running records of writing progress

It is surprisingly difficult to take running records of a young child writing with the teacher's assistance. In a classroom the teacher is either interacting with the child or allowing the child to interact with informed others to help the child as s/he writes. In several research studies, students have tried to devise ways of recording what occurs in such observations but it turns out to be much more difficult than taking running records of reading. In a report that appeared in *The Reading Teacher* (May 1991) there is a record that traces a child's progress in the first ten weeks of school. That record had to be simplified, leaving out many things that the observer saw. In that record it is possible to show the child becoming a more independent writer in a few weeks. It is also an interesting account of what the teacher was trying to achieve as she worked alongside the child. Those who wish to take observation records of children writing in authentic situations in interaction with teachers, children, and other helpers should be warned to be ready for complicated sequences of behavior.

Writing a story

An older child who can write fifty or more words is too competent for the use of the Writing Vocabulary task in either Spanish or English. S/he should be encouraged to write a story of several sentences or paragraphs (with as little help as possible) to provide a basis for grouping or categorizing children's stories according to selected criteria. To assess change over time an earlier record for one child can be compared with a later one, and the progress made should be clearly articulated.

Spelling

Older children can be given a spelling test that usually yields a normalized score. Spelling tests are often constructed with particular sets of words—regular words, irregular words, spelling "demons," foreign words, or words from different language roots (e.g., *kiosko* in Spanish), etc. Such constraints must be taken into account when interpreting the child's observed behavior, and such behavior should not be generalized to the writing of words outside the set of words used in the observation task.

Useful information from spelling observations is the evidence that is provided by watching the child at work and noting her/his strengths (words known, strategies that work, analogies that are tried). After the child has reached the upper threshold of her/his spelling achieve-

ESCRITURA ACUMULADA DE VOCABULARIO

Nombre: _____   Fecha de Nacimiento _____

Números de palabras el niño/a puede escribir																							
52																							
50																							
48																							
46																							
44																							
42																							
40																							
38																							
36																							
34																							
32																							
30																							
28																							
26																							
24																							
22																							
20																							
18																							
16																							
14																							
12																							
10																							
8																							
6																							
4																							
2																							
0																							
Fecha																							

Fechas de observaciones

ment (where mostly correct spelling passes over to mostly incorrect spelling), the incorrect responses provide evidence of risk-taking, control of spelling patterns, the use of analogy, the rule-guided behavior, and also of gaps, confusions, or interfering or unproductive strategies. Sources in Spanish include the *Lengua Española*, *DOL—Español*, and *Ortografía* published by Santillana or other language arts guides that are published as a part of commercially produced Spanish reading materials.

OÍR Y REGISTRAR SONIDOS EN PALABRAS—TAREA DE DICTADO (*HEARING AND RECORDING SOUNDS IN WORDS—DICTATION TASK*)

This observation task was called dictation by Clay (1989) because the teacher asks the child to record a dictated sentence. But the child's product is scored by counting the child's representation of the sounds (phonemes) by letters (graphemes). Being able to hear the sounds in the words you want to write is an authentic task—a task one encounters in the real world rather than one devised merely for the purpose of testing. This observation task directs the attention of teachers and children to phonemic awareness, a current emphasis in the research literature. Phonemic awareness is important in learning to read in both English and Spanish.

School entrants can speak a language and need to learn to read and write that language if possible. In some cases this language is English, in some it is Spanish or other languages. They need to work out how every aspect of their spoken language relates to messages in print. Children need to learn how the language knowledge they already have can help them to read and write messages. One of the things they already know is how to use most of the sounds of their language. But how to work with the phonemes of a language is only one of the many things readers and writers need to know.

Recent research in teaching reading in English has made it clear that we must pay attention to four aspects of how the sounds of a language are represented in print (Clay 1993).

1 Children have to learn to hear the sounds buried within words and this is not an easy task.
2 Children have to learn to visually discriminate the symbols we use in print.
3 Children have to learn to link single symbols and *clusters* of symbols with the sounds they represent.

4 Children have to learn that there are many alternatives and exceptions in the system of putting sounds into print in any language.

The above aspects of how the sounds of English are represented in print are equally important in learning to read and write in Spanish. Further, these four concepts represent universal concepts about phoneme/grapheme relationships that assist readers from one language as they learn to read and write in a second language.

Children begin to work on relationships among a few things they have learned long before they learn all there is to know about letters and sounds. You do not have to know all the members of a set before you can work out some of the set's characteristics. Also, as Clay discovered while doing research in English, while some teachers are tediously teaching one letter-sound link after another in reading or writing, some children have already begun to read or write using bigger chunks of information. Clay makes the following assertions about "information chunking" among children learning to read and write:

- It is more efficient to work with larger chunks, and so they do!
- Sometimes it is more efficient to work with relationships than items of knowledge (like letters or words), and so they do!
- Often it is efficient to use a vague sense of a rule, and so they do!

They do not wait for the teacher to get through all her lessons on sounds before they begin working with larger chunks and relationships. Research on the teaching of reading and writing in Spanish has determined that the same type of "information chunking" occurs when students are learning to read and write in Spanish.

A useful observation task to capture the child's control of sound to letter links is "hearing sounds in words." The teacher tells the child a sentence to be written. The child is encouraged to write what s/he can hear in the words dictated. What s/he does not hear will not get recorded. Scores show how successful the child was at hearing the sounds in the words and finding a possible way of recording those sounds in English using the English spelling system, or in Spanish using the Spanish spelling system.

Administration

The observer selects one of the four alternative sentences to use in this observation task (p. 97). This child is given credit for every sound (phoneme) that s/he writes correctly, even though the whole word may not be correctly spelled. The scores give some indication of the child's ability to analyze the word s/he hears or says and to find a way of recording in letters the sounds that s/he can hear. Use an alternative form for retesting children. As with other observation tasks, the Spanish guidelines for administration are written in boldface and the English are included in italics.

Diga:

"Te voy a leer un cuento. Cuando termine de leerlo una vez, volveré a leerlo otra vez muy despacio para que tú puedas escribir las palabras del cuento." (Lea el cuento con fluidez.) "Algunas de las palabras son difíciles. Dilas despacito a tí mismo y piensa de cómo las podrías escribir. Ahora, empieza a escribir las palabras."

Say:

"I am going to read you a story. When I have read it through once I will read it again very slowly so that you can write down the words in the story." (Read the story at normal speed.) "Some of the words are hard. Say them slowly and think how you can write them. Start writing the words now.'

Diga las palabras despacio, palabra por palabra. Si el estudiante tiene dificultad, diga:

"Tú, dilo despacito. ¿Cómo empezarías a escribirlo? ¿Qué sonido oyes? ¿Qué más puedes oír?"

Dictate slowly, word by word. When the child comes to a problem word say:

"You say it slowly. How would you start to write it? What can you hear?" Then add, "What else can you hear?"

Si el estudiante no puede terminar la palabra, diga:

"Vamos a dejar de escribir esta palabra. La siguiente palabra es . . ." Apunte a donde escribir la próxima palabra si eso le auyda al estudiante.

If the child cannot complete the word say:

"We'll leave that word. The next one is . . ." Point to where to write the next word if this helps the child.

Support the child with comments like these to keep the child working at the task.

When retesting, use an alternative form to avoid prac-

tice effects. The alternative forms for this task are listed on page 97.

Recording

Use the form on page 100 for recording. Write the text below the child's version after the task is finished. Some examples are included below.

dise	biene	parce	trn	t
dice	viene	parque	tren	tengo

Scoring

The rules for scoring given here are necessary to ensure reliability and validity when the task is used for measurement of progress or change.

While initially the child's progress will be in the area of "hearing and recording sounds in words," as s/he moves toward more control over writing we must expect her/him to be learning something about the orthography (the spelling rules and patterns) of the language.

Score one point for each sound (phoneme) the child has analyzed and recorded that is numbered 1 to 39 on the examples (p. 97) and record the total out of 39.

There can be no set of rules for scoring that will cover the ingenuity found in children's attempts. Scores are advised to be conservative rather than liberal in applying the following scoring criteria if comparable results are to be achieved across different scorers.

The teacher who is a sensitive observer would note any partially correct responses that tell a great deal about the cutting edge of the child's knowledge. Such qualitative information is very important for planning the kind of help to offer the child.

There are many arguments about developmental change from partially correct to correct responding. Recorders do not always agree on how to score partially correct responding and so for a reliable measuring instrument, only the correct responding criteria for scoring can be recommended.

Additions and omissions

If a letter does not have a number underneath it in the scoring standards on page 97, then it receives *no* score.

$$\underline{N}\ \underline{o}\underline{s}\quad \underline{v}\underline{a}\underline{m}\underline{o}\underline{s}\quad a\quad \underline{s}\underline{u}\underline{b}\underline{i}\underline{r.}$$

The *a* receives no score since it does not have a line under it.

Additions do not affect scoring as long as numbered letters are included.

Disce   Score 4
dice

Capital letters
Capital letters are acceptable substitutions for lower letters and vice versa.

Substitutions
Given what it being observed in this task, it makes sense to accept a response when the sound analysis has been a useful one, even though the child has used graphemes that can record the sound but in this particular case the spelling is incorrect.

As a general principle substitute letters are acceptable if, in Spanish, the sound is sometimes recorded in that way. The following substitutions which count as correct are:

c/qu/k	parce/parke	kasa
	parque	casa
ll/y/i	yega/iega	llo/io
	llega	yo
s/c/z	caza	ce	dise
	casa	se	dice
b/v	biene	bamos	
	viene	vamos	
j/g	gugar		
	jugar		

In addition to the above, in Spanish there are many dialectical differences. If this is the case, have the child pronounce the word after you as you are dictating. Note whether the child's pronunciation matches his/her spelling. Words with omitted beginning or ending sounds still count as incorrect, even though the child's spelling matches his/her pronunciation.

Changes in letter order
Where the child has made a change in letter order take one mark off for that word. For example:

$$\frac{es}{se} \quad 2\text{-}1 = 1 \qquad \frac{vamso}{vamos} \quad 5 - 1 = 4$$

Reversed letters
Reversed letters are not correct if they could represent a different letter. However, they are correct if they could not represent a different letter. Examples of reversals that are counted as correct on this task include *s*, *c*, *r*, and *z*. Examples of reversals that are counted as incorrect are *b*/*d*, and *p*/*q*.

Making notes on other observations
It is important that the observer also make notes on the following:

• any sequencing errors
• the omission of sounds
• unusual use of space on the page
• unusual placement of letters within word
• partially correct attempts
• 'good' confusions.

Any of these may tell the teacher something about what the learner knows and how the teacher may support some shift in performance.

Scoring standards
Use the scoring standard for the form you selected (A, B, C, Ch). See page 97.

Dictation Sentences from English Observation Survey:
I have a big dog at home. Today I am going to take him to school.
Mum has gone up to the shop. She will get milk and bread.
I can see the red boat that we are going to have a ride in.
The bus is coming. It will stop here to let me get on.
The boy is riding his bike. He can go very fast on it.

Oraciones del Dictado en Español (Spanish Dictation Sentences with English Translations):
Tengo un perro en la casa. Lo llevo al parque conmigo.
(*I have a dog at home. I take him to the park with me.*)
Papá está en casa. Dice que vamos a jugar a la pelota.
(*Dad is at home. He says we are going to play ball.*)
Yo tengo una gata café. Le gusta dormir en mi cama.
(*I have a brown cat. She likes to sleep in my bed.*)
Ya viene el tren. Se va a parar aquí. Nos vamos a subir.
(*Here comes the train. It is going to stop here. We're going to get on.*)

RESULTADOS DEL DICTADO

Texto alternativo

Seleccione una de las siguientes formas: A, B, C, Ch.

Forma A Tengo un perro en la casa.
1 2 3 4 5 6 7 8 9 10 11 12 13 14 15 16 17 18 19

Lo llevo al parque conmigo.
20 21 22 23 24 25 26 27 28 29 30 31 32 33 34 35 36 37 38 39

Forma B Papá está en casa.
1 2 3 4 5 6 7 8 9 10 11 12 13 14

Dice que vamos a jugar a la pelota.
15 16 17 18 19 20 21 22 23 24 25 26 27 28 29 30 31 32 33 34 35 36 37 38 39

Forma C Yo tengo una gata café.
1 2 3 4 5 6 7 8 9 10 11 12 13 14 15 16 17 18

Le gusta dormir en mi cama.
19 20 21 22 23 24 25 26 27 28 29 30 31 32 33 34 35 36 37 38 39

Forma Ch Ya viene el tren. Se va a parar
1 2 3 4 5 6 7 8 9 10 11 12 13 14 15 16 17 18 19 20 21 22 23

aquí. Nos vamos a subir.
24 25 26 27 28 29 30 31 32 33 34 35 36 37 38 39

Research Group	Oír y Registrar Sonidos en Palabras—Tarea de Dictado (Hearing and Recording Sounds in Words—Dictation Task) Normalized scores—Stanine Groups								
	Stanine Group	1	2	3	4	5	6	7	8	9
Urban Children in first grade in 1991–92 from Arizona, Texas, and Illinois	Fall 1991 N = 282	0	1–3	4–5	6–11	12–18	19–26	27–33	34–37	38–39
	Mid-Year	0–4	5–12	13–19	20–29	30–33	34–36	37	38	39
	Spring 1992 N = 202	0–6	7–14	15–21	22–31	32–35	36–37	38	39	39

Validity: Correlation with Aprenda Spanish Reading Achievement Test for 282 children in fall 1991; $r = .70$ Correlation with Aprenda Spanish Reading Achievement Test for 202 children in spring 1992; $r = .60$ (Escamilla 1992)

Reliability: 282 children in fall 1991, $r = .96$; Cronbach's Alpha Analysis 202 children in spring 1992, $r = .95$; (Escamilla 1992)

Note: In order to determine a midyear scoring range, the fall and spring scores on each observation task were averaged in the following manner: $\dfrac{Score\ F\ +\ Score\ S}{2}$

Observing change over time

Susan Robinson and Barbara Watson devised and used the Hearing Sounds in Words observations during the development of the Reading Recovery program in English (Clay 1993). They proved to be valuable indicators of change over time of a child's ability to go from the analysis of sounds to spoken words to written forms for representing these sounds. In that sense this is not a true dictation or spelling test. The same type of task has been found to be valuable in observing change over time in children who are learning to read in Spanish (Escamilla 1992).

In the example included below, Javier was given the Spanish task of Oír y Registrar Sonidos en Palabras (Hearing and Recording Sounds in Words) in October 1991 and again in February 1992. Since a teacher is supposed to give an alternative form of the test, Javier was given Forma A (Form A) in the fall and Forma B (Form B) when he discontinued the Descubriendo La Lectura program sixteen weeks later. In Javier's writing sample below, his progress across time is readily visible. In the first sample (fall 1991), Javier demonstrates what he knows.

1 He can write some capital letters—some of which represent sounds he heard in the dictated sentence.

2 He can hear and record some sounds that occur at the end of words (e.g., o at the end of tengo; n at the end of en).

3 He can hear and record some sounds at the beginning of words (e.g., l at the beginning of the word la; k at the beginning of the word casa; l at the beginning of the word lo; and y at the beginning of the word llevo)

4 He can hear and record some sounds in the middle of words (e.g., k in the middle of parque).

By the end of February when he is once again given the task of hearing and recording sounds from a dictated sentence, he has become much more sophisticated in the way that he records sounds. He now leaves spaces between words, he can record whole words from dictation, and his recording more closely resembles standard conventions used in writing and spelling Spanish. In addition, he is beginning to use punctuation and accent marks.

JAVIER'S SAMPLE DICTATION

| Fall 1991 | Score 7 |

Tengo un perro en la casa. Lo llevo al parque conmigo.

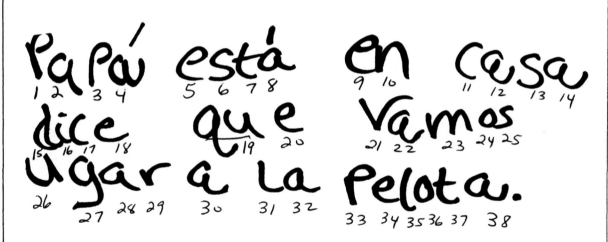

| Feb. 1992 | Score 38 |

Papá está en casa. Dice que vamos a jugar a la pelota.

Hearing and Recording Sounds in Words (Dictation Task),
comparison of an early and later testing.

OÍR Y REGISTRAR SONIDOS EN PALABRAS (DICTADO)
HOJA DE OBSERVACIÓN

Fecha _____

Nombre _____ _____ Edad _____ RESULTADO [   ]

Observador _____ Fecha de Nacimiento _____ GRUPO ESTANINA [   ]

Doble el encabezado hacia atrás antes de que el niño use la hoja.

COMENTARIO:

8 | SUMMARIZING THE RESULTS OF THE OBSERVATION SURVEY

Kathy Escamilla
Ana María Andrade
Amelia G. M. Basurto
Olivia A. Ruiz
with Marie Clay

In the summary of *El Instrumento de Observación* (Observation Survey) the teacher brings together what s/he has observed. S/he describes what the child can do and what is partially known at the boundaries of her/his knowledge, as it were. Teachers should decide for which children they need a full analysis of *El Instrumento de Observación*. They may, for example:

- make notes on teaching points for competent children
- make brief summaries for a broad average group
- produce detailed write-ups for children whose progress really puzzles them.

From the detailed information the instrumento (survey) yields, a first step toward an integrative summary is to summarize the results under the headings listed on two Hojas Para el Resumen de la Observación (Observation Survey Summary Sheets) as follows:

Book reading
Transfer the detail of the running records obtained at three levels and the analysis of cues used and cues neglected on to Sheet 1 of the Observation Survey Summary Sheet if you are using English (p. 107) or Hoja 1 de La Hoja para el Resumen de la Observación if you are using Spanish (p. 109).

Other observation tasks
Summarize the results of the other observation tasks and data on to either the Spanish Sheet 1 (p. 107) or the English Sheet 1 (p. 109).

Analysis of strategies used by the child
On the second sheet of either the Observation Survey Summary Sheet if s/he is using English (p. 108) or La Hoja para el Resumen de la Observación if s/he is using Spanish (p. 110), the teacher makes an analysis of the ways in which this child approaches and solves problems or new challenges. The teacher completes each section under useful and problem strategies on text, with words and with letters, using the questions on pages 102 and 103. Comments should be made on the child's performance in relation to each of the following six topics:

- Useful strategies on text
- Problem strategies on text
- Useful strategies with words
- Problem strategies with words
- Useful strategies with letters and sounds, separately and in clusters.
- Problem strategies with letters and sounds, separately and in clusters

LOOKING FOR STRATEGIES

There are several reasons for this approach to summarizing *El Instrumento de Observación*.

- Any language is organized hierarchically on several levels. Only three have been selected here—text (a general term to stand for phrase, sentence, or larger text), word level, and letter level.
- It has been argued (Clay 1991) that although the reader appears to have stored many items of knowl-

edge s/he has also learned strategies for working with the information in print—ways of finding it, storing it, filing it, retrieving it, and linking or cross-referencing one kind of information with another kind.

Good observation rather than modern linguistic theory led a talented reading clinician, Grace Fernald (1943), to formulate these statements about the relationships of letters, words, and texts in reading:

> Groups of words must be the focus of attention in reading. Attending to the words as separate units, as in word-by-word reading, loses important meanings. The meaning of a word can vary with the group in which it occurs or, in another way, a group of words has a certain meaning. The sentence is the context in which the meaning of the word group is confirmed. The known word is the unit at which level the precision of the word group is usually confirmed. For the unknown, unfamiliar, forgotten or misperceived word the reader's attention must go to clusters of letters or even to individual letters but whether these are right or not must be confirmed at the level of the word unit.

She insisted, therefore, that in writing the word always be written as a unit and in reading words always be used in context.

The questions listed in the next section helped some teachers to describe the reading strategies young children use. Some examples of what is meant by reading strategies are given in Katy's records in English (p. 105), and in Javier's records in Spanish (p. 106). Further information is provided in the case reports of Mary in English and Javier in Spanish (pp. 104 and 111).

USEFUL STRATEGIES ON TEXT

Look at the Running Record of book reading where the child is performing adequately (90 to 100 percent accuracy) and try to find some evidence of how effectively s/he works with the sequences of cues. Also look at Conceptos del Texto Impreso (*Concepts About Print*) items. Use these questions as a guide to your analysis of the records.

Location and movement
Does s/he control directional movement?
  –left to right?

  –top to bottom?
  –return sweep?
Does s/he locate particular cues in print? Which cues?
Does s/he read word by word? If so, is this a new achievement (+) or an old habit (−)?

Language
Does s/he control language well?
Does s/he read for meaning?
Does s/he control book language?
Does s/he have a good memory for text?
Does s/he read for the precise message?

Behavior at difficulties
Does s/he seek help?
Does s/he try again?
Does s/he search for further cues? How?
(Note unusual behaviors.)

Error substitutions
Do the error substitutions the child uses make sense with the previous text? (Sentido/Significado) (*Meaning*)
Do they continue an acceptable sentence in Spanish? (Estructura) (*Structure*)
Could they occur in grammar for that sentence, up to that word?
Is the child getting to new words from known words by analogy? For example, in English from *name* to *game* or from *play* and *jump* to *plump*, or in Spanish from *casa* to *pasa* or from *llave* and *amar* to *llamar*?
Do some of the letters in the error match with letters in the text? (Use señales visuales o gráficos [*visual or graphic cues*].)

Self-correction
Does s/he return to the beginning of the line?
Does s/he return back a few words?
Does s/he repeat the word only?
Does s/he read on to the end of the line (a difficult and confusing strategy for young readers)?
Does s/he repeat only the initial sound of a word?
(Note unusual behaviors.)

Cross-checking strategies
At an early stage of text reading, does s/he
–ignore discrepancies?
–check language with movement?
–check language with visual cues?

–try to make language, movement, and visual cues line up?

USEFUL STRATEGIES WITH WORDS

Check Conceptos del Texto Impreso (CTI), *(Concepts About Print)*; Lectura Actual del Texto *(Text Reading)*; Escritura de Vocabulario *(Writing Vocabulary)*; Oír y Registrar Sonidos en Palabras—Dictado *(Hearing and Recording Sounds in Words—Dictation)*, and Prueba de Palabras *(Word Test)*.

The visual features of words
On CTI recognizes line rearrangement
On CTI recognizes word rearrangement
On CTI recognizes that the first and last letters are re-arranged
On CTI recognizes that the medial letters are rearranged
On text can attend to detail
Responds to initial letters
Responds to initial and final letters
Relates to some prior visual or writing experience of that word
On Escritura de Vocabulario *(Writing Vocabulary)* knows some words in every detail.

Los sonidos de palabras *(the sounds of words)*
Can hear the individual words in a sentence
Can articulate words slowly
Can break up words into sounds (as in a dictated sentence)
Attempts to write new words using a sound analysis
Builds a syllabic framework for a new word
Knows that vowels are consistent
Knows that consonants are difficult and works at them
Rereads what s/he has written, carefully.

USEFUL STRATEGIES WITH LETTERS

Check Conceptos del Texto Impreso (CTI), *(Concepts About Print)*; Lectura Actual del Texto *(Text Reading)*; Escritura de Vocabulario *(Writing Vocabulary)*; Oír y Registrar Sonidos en Palabras—Dictado *(Hearing and Recording Sounds in Words—Dictation)*, and Prueba de Palabras *(Word Test)*.

Movement
Does the child form (write) some letters easily?
Does s/he form many letters without a copy?

Visual
Which letters can s/he identify?
Could s/he detect an error because of a mismatch of letters?
(Which letters were difficult?)
(Which letters were confused one with another?)

Sounds
How does a child attempt a word in the Oír y Registrar Sonidos en Palabras—Dictado *(Hearing Sounds in Words—Dictation)* task?
Does s/he articulate it slowly?
Can s/he isolate the first sound or syllable of a word that s/he hears?
Can s/he give other words that start with the same sound?
Can s/he make/read/write other words that end with the same spelling pattern or inflection?

SUMMARIZING *EL INSTRUMENTO*

The method of summarizing the survey results adopted in the summary sheet is incomplete in that it does not tell the teacher how to search for those strategies that relate one level of linguistic organization to another, letters to words, and words to their meaningful contexts. Research has not addressed many of these questions in ways the observing teacher can use at this point. We do not yet know much about such nonverbal metacognitive strategies.

Writing up el resumén de la observación *(survey summary)*
Using only the evidence you have been reporting describe in a few lines the child's current way of responding. Point out what s/he can and cannot do on text reading and text writing. Indicate how her/his strategies (the ways in which s/he works) on word and letter levels help or hinder her/his getting messages from text. This statement is crucial for the teacher because it forces her/him to bring all the information on the reader who has been observed together in an overview statement. This could be the starting point of a program of individual help.

The way in which Katy's teacher and Humberto's teacher wrote about their strategies on texts, words, and letters in the summary that followed the Observation Survey is shown on pages 105 and 106. Katy's and Humberto's literacy achievement after one year in school was sufficiently low to warrant their referral to an early intervention program.

WHAT DOES THIS SUMMARY MEAN FOR THE CHILD IN THE CLASSROOM?

The teacher will have gathered much information about the child during the administration of the observation tasks. (S/he will have more understanding of these many observations if s/he has pulled together the collective message in the Resumen de la Observación or survey summary.) What does *El Instrumento de Observación* or the observation survey now imply for her/his classroom practice? It is useful to ask the following questions:

Books?
What does *El Instrumento de Observación* or the survey imply about the way new books are introduced to this child? Is a rich introduction required? Or is the child able to approach a new book with minimal preparation or guidance? Are there indications that other types of text need to be part of this child's reading? Do the books you are using support this child, allowing her/him to use what s/he knows in the service of trying new texts?

Writing?
Is there any aspect of writing that requires special attention? Does the child analyze the sounds in words and try to find ways of writing them? Does the child ask for feedback on her/his attempts? Does the child have a core vocabulary of high frequency words to support her/his story writing? What kinds of help does your classroom provide for the child to get to new words on her/his own?

Your program?
Do the results from several children tell you anything about (a) the emphases of your program and (b) the things you tend to be overlooking? Consistent patterns across children in reading and writing behaviors may provide evidence of emphases that you never intended or confusions you had never thought of. Are there confusions to be got rid of? Are there new things to which you need to draw children's attention? Do you have to think about more helpful and supportive texts? Do you need to provide more individual help for children to get their composed stories down on paper?

Next strategies?
What changes in strategies would you wish to see these children making over the next three months of instruction? Will you expect them to be more independent of

you and how is this to be achieved? An observation summary sheet for recording multiple testing is shown on page 112 in English and page 113 in Spanish.

TWO EXAMPLES OF SURVEY SUMMARIES (ONE IN ENGLISH/ ONE IN SPANISH)

I Mary aged 6:0—early reading stage

Initial testing: 4.5.77
Initial status: Early reading—one-line texts.

1 Book reading
Mary read three Caption Books: I Am Big (seen), The Bear Family (seen) and I Am Little (unseen) with 94, 87, 75 percent accuracy and 0:3, 1:5, 0:8 self-correction rates.

2 Observation task results
Mary's score on Letter Identification was 34/54, on Concepts About Print 13/24, on the Word Tests 3/15 and 0/30, on Writing Vocabulary 2 and on the Hearing Sounds in Words task 8/37.

3 Useful strategies on text
Mary uses fluent book language. She moves across the print from left to right with return sweep.

Problem strategies on text
Mary's fluent language response overrides visual and locating cues. Under the tester's monitoring she can locate word-by-word and can attend to the words she knows in print (*I*, *am*, *is here*), but when she works independently her language response is too fluent to allow any integration of cues. Her self-correction rates are low. She does not attend to letter cues. Her miscues had zero graphic correspondence.

4 Useful strategies with words
Mary recognized *I*, *here*, *am* in isolation. She wrote the sentence:

"I si a May" (for I am Mary)

She analyzed some initial sounds (*for, have, big, home*) on the Hearing Sounds in Words task.

Problem strategies with words
Mary does not attend to words while reading unless asked to "Look carefully and read with your finger."

Useful strategies on text:

Katy controls directional movement and one-to-one correspondence. She uses visual cues of initial letters, meaning cues sometimes and to a lesser extent structure cues. She does some rerunning and repeating to confirm and/or check. She is able to cross-check language with visual cues and self-corrects as a result.

Problem strategies on text:

She does not control book language well and at the hard level, structure and meaning tend to be overriden by visual cues. She does not rerun or seek help at difficulties. She does not read for the precise message. She uses minimal cross-checking of meaning, structure and visual cues, and minimal self-correction.

Useful strategies with words:

On text she is able to attend to detail especially initial letters. In Hearing Sounds In Words she can hear the individual words in a sentence and isolate and record some initial, final and dominant consonants in words. She has a small core of high frequency words which she can write.

Problem strategies with words:

On CAP she does not recognise line, word or letter rearrangement. On text she doesn't attend to letter detail consistently especially medial and final letters. In writing and hearing sounds she cannot always hear and record the correct consonant, and there is occasional sequencing difficulty.

Useful strategies with letters:

Katy identifies letters dominantly by alphabet response but occasionally gives a word or sound response. She can analyse some sound-to-letter relationships and some letter-to-sound relationships on text. She can write some letters with reasonable ease and form many letters without a copy.

Problem strategies with letters:

She does not always use her letter knowledge to identify the precise detail of a word. She confuses some letters in Letter Identification. On CAP she failed to locate both examples of upper/lower case correspondence, one and two letters and the capital letter.

SUMMARY

Katy is reading at Book Level 3. She has control over early strategies of directionality and one-to-one matching of words and seems to be able to locate some known and unknown words on text. She tends to use visual cues dominantly and sometimes uses meaning cues but does not always attend to structure cues to elicit the precise meaning of text. Limited repetition and rerunning and minimal self-correction appear to indicate she is not always monitoring and using strategies to cross-check for the precise detail of print. She can recognise and write some words and can analyse some letters from sound to letter but is not able to process and integrate this information effectively on text and in writing.

SIGNATURE:

How Katy's teacher summarized
Katy's Observation Survey.

Estrategias útiles del texto

Humberto contola el movimiento direccional y el pareo de uno a uno. Utiliza las claves de significado y estructura; a un grado menor, utiliza las claves visuales, usando frecuentemente la letra principiante de la palabra. Hace un repaso del texto con el fin de confirmar o verificar.

Estrategias problemáticas del texto

No controla bien el uso de las claves visuales, y a un nivel difícil, tiende prevalecer el uso de claves de significado y estructura sobre las claves visuales. No lee con el fin de entender el mensaje preciso. A un grado minimo, comprenda las claves de signifacdo, estructura y visuales; y como resultado, autocorrige su trabajo.

Estrategias útiles acerca de las palabras

Humberto conoce la diferencia entre palabra y letra. En la tarea de Oír y Anotar Sonidos en las Palabras, puede oír y anotar palabras individuales, alguna letras principiantes y con más frecuencia, las vocales. Tiene una pequeña base de palabras útiles que puede escribir con fluidez.

Estrategias problemáticas acerca de las palabras

No atiende consistentemente a los detalles de las letras en el texto, especialmente en las letras del centro y finales de las palabras. Aunque puede analizar algunos sonidos, y a veces atender a los detalles visuales de la escritura, no puede aplicar estas destrezas a las palabras del texto.

Estrategias útiles acerca de las letras

Identifica por nombre, la mayoría de las letras y a un grado menor, las identifica por palabra o sonido. Reconoce las letras mayúsculas y minúsculas. Al escribir palabras puede oír y anotar con más frecuencia, vocales, letras principiantes o finales de una palabra.

Estrategias problemáticas acerca de las letras

Humberto rara vez, aplica su conocimiento de las letras para identificar el detalle preciso de una palabra. En la tarea de Identificación de Letras, confunde las letras b/d y p/q. Al escribir palabras, a veces escribe algunas letras al revés.

RESUMEN

Humberto lee al Nivel del libro 3. Tiene control sobre las estrategias principiantes del movimiento direccional y el pareo de uno a uno. Parece poder encontrar en el texto, algunas palabras conocidas y palabras desconocidas. Principalmente, tiende usar las claves de significado y de estructura para determinar el sentido del texto, y a veces, atiende a las claves visuales. La limitada repetición, el repaso, y el uso mínimo de la autocorreción parecen indicar que Humberto no siempre observa cuidadosamente ni usa las estrategias de comprobación que determinan los detalles precisos del texto. Puede reconocer y escribir algunas palabras, y a través de la relación entre el sonido y la letra, puede analizar las letras; pero no puede usar este procedimiento ni puede intregrar esta información eficazmente en el texto, ni por escrito.

FIRMA:

OBSERVATION SURVEY SUMMARY SHEET

Recommended for survey checks after one year of instruction

Name: _____ Date: _____ D. of B. _____ Age: ____ yrs ____ mths

School: _____ Recorder: _____

Text Titles	Running words / Error	Error rate	Accuracy	Self-correction rate
1. Easy _____	_____	1: _____	_____ %	1: _____
2. Instructional _____	_____	1: _____	_____ %	1: _____
3. Hard _____	_____	1: _____	_____ %	1: _____

Directional movement _____

Analysis of Errors and Self-corrections
Cues used or neglected [Meaning (M) Structure or Syntax (S) Visual (V)]

Easy _____

Instructional _____
_____

Hard _____
_____

Cross-checking on cues (Note that this behaviour changes over time)
_____
_____

LETTER IDENTIFICATION

	54

CONCEPTS ABOUT PRINT   *SAND*   *STONES*

	24

WORD TEST (CLAY)   LIST A _____ LIST B _____ LIST C _____

	15

OTHER READING TEST _____

WRITING SAMPLE	WRITING VOCABULARY	HEARING SOUNDS IN WORDS (DICTATION)	STORY	SPELLING
Language: Message: Direction:		A B C D E 37		

Useful strategies on text:

Problem strategies on text:

Useful strategies with words:

Problem strategies with words:

Useful strategies with letters:

Problem strategies with letters:

SUMMARY:

SIGNATURE: _____

RESUMEN DEL INSTRUMENTO DE OBSERVACIÓN
Se recomienda para hacer controles del instrumento después de un año de instrucción

Nombre _____ Fecha _____ Fecha de Nacimiento _____ Edad ___ Años ___ Meses ___

Escuela _____ Observador _____

Títulos del Texto	Palabras Actuales Error	Proporción de Errores	Exactitud	Proporción de Autocorrección
1. Fácil _____	_____	1: _____	_____ %	1: _____
2. Requiere Enseñanza _____	_____	1: _____	_____ %	1: _____
3. Difícil _____	_____	1: _____	_____ %	1: _____

Movimiento directivo _____

Análisis de Errores y de Autocorrecciones

Claves utilizadas o desatendidas [Significado (S)   Estructura o Sintáxis (E)   Visual (V)]

Fácil _____

Requiere Enseñanza _____
_____

Difícil _____
_____

Cotejo de claves (Observe que este comportamiento cambia con el tiempo)
_____
_____

IDENTIFICACIÓN DE LETRAS

$\overline{61}$

CONCEPTOS DEL TEXTO IMPRESO   *LAS PIEDRAS*   *ARENA*

$\overline{25}$

PRUEBA DE PALABRA (CLAY)   LISTA A _____ LISTA B _____ LISTA C _____ $\overline{20}$

OTRA PRUEBA DE LECTURA _____

MUESTRA DE ESCRITURA	ESCRITURA DE VOCABULARIO	OÍR SONIDOS EN PALABRAS (DICTADO)	CUENTO	ORTOGRAFÍA
Lenguaje: Mensaje: Dirección		A B C Ch D $\overline{39}$		

Estrategias útiles en texto:

Estrategias difíciles en texto:

Estrategias útiles con palabras:

Estrategias difíciles con palabras:

Estrategias útiles con letras:

Estrategias difíciles con letras:

RESUMEN:

FIRMA: _____

Locating in print and coordinating finger and speech in word-by-word reading is a difficult coordination for her to make.

5 Useful strategies with letters

Mary identified 34/54 letters by name. She knows some sound-to-letter relationships.

Problem strategies with letters

Mary's long list of confused letters implies that she does not know how to search for ways of distinguishing similar letter shapes (i.e., how to visually discriminate between the pairs).

$$\frac{I}{L} \quad \frac{F}{E} \quad \frac{I}{T} \quad \frac{j}{f} \quad \frac{q}{u} \quad \frac{g}{y} \quad \frac{i}{I} \quad \frac{r}{q} \quad \frac{b}{d} \quad \frac{h}{n} \quad \frac{k}{x} \quad \frac{j}{i} \quad \frac{b}{p} \quad \frac{b}{g} \quad \frac{O}{Q}$$

Summary

Mary has made some progress with the use of visual cues but her fluent language overrides visual cues and prevents word-by-word reading. Discrepancies do not signal to her to recheck and self-correct.

II Javier aged 6:9—first reading books

Initial testing: 9.8.77
Initial status: First Readers

1 Lectura de Texto

Javier leyó *La gallinita roja* (conocida) con 98% de exactitud y una proporción de 0:1 en la autocorrección. También leyó el cuento *EL TRAJE NUEVO DEL EMPERADOR* con 79% de exactitud y una proporción de 1:3 en la autocorrección.

2 Resultados de las tareas de observación

El resultado de la tarea de Identificación de Letras fue 31/61; Conceptos del Texto Impreso—19/25; Prueba de Palabras—5/15; Escritura de Vocabulario—7 y el resultado de la tarea de Oír y Registrar Sonidos en Palabras—11/37.

3 Estrategias Útiles en texto

Javier predice el significado del texto usando las claves de los dibujos y usando el pareo de uno a uno; a veces analiza algunas letras principiantes a través de la relación entre el sonido y la letra. Se autocorrige, usando el pareo de uno a uno y usando algunas de sus palabras conocidas.

Estrategias difíciles en texto

Sus errores en el texto, son aceptables semántica y sintácticamente, pero no ortográficamente. Javier es muy distraído y trata de evitar la tarea de leer.

4 Estrategias útiles con palabras

Identificó algunas palabras aisladas. Escribió siete palabras. Utiliza una pequeña base de palabras al leer. Puede analizar algunos sonidos de las palabras.

Estrategias difíciles con palabras

La habilidad de recordar palabras es difícil para Javier. Su buen lenguaje oral domina su conocimiento de palabras al leer un texto nuevo.

5 Estrategias útiles con letras

Identificó por nombre 31 letras. Puede analizar los sonidos principiantes y algunos sonidos del centro de las palabras. Al leer, a veces puede analizar la letra principiante a través de la relación entre el sonido y la letra.

Estrategias difíciles con letras

Javier confundió más letras en la tarea de Identificación de Letras

$$\frac{n}{u} \quad \frac{u}{y} \quad \frac{x}{z} \quad \frac{z}{x} \quad \frac{E}{F}$$

que en la tarea del Escritura de Vocabulario $\frac{W}{M}$, y necesita aprender cómo controlar estas confusiones.

Resumen

Javier ha progresado en las destrezas principiantes de la lectura, pero su edad, el ser tan distraído, su dificultad en recordar palabras a vista, y uso dominante del lenguaje oral al leer, le ha impedido progresar rápidamente en la lectura.

OBSERVATION SUMMARY FOR MULTIPLE TESTINGS

Name: _____

Date of Birth: _____

School: _____

SUMMARY OF RUNNING RECORD

	Text Titles	Running words / Error	Error rate	Accuracy	Self-correction rate

Initial Test   Date: _____

1. Easy _____ _____ 1: _____ _____ % 1: _____
2. Instructional _____ _____ 1: _____ _____ % 1: _____
3. Hard _____ _____ 1: _____ _____ % 1: _____

Retest   Date: _____

1. Easy _____ _____ 1: _____ _____ % 1: _____
2. Instructional _____ _____ 1: _____ _____ % 1: _____
3. Hard _____ _____ 1: _____ _____ % 1: _____

Further Test   Date: _____

1. Easy _____ _____ 1: _____ _____ % 1: _____
2. Instructional _____ _____ 1: _____ _____ % 1: _____
3. Hard _____ _____ 1: _____ _____ % 1: _____

TESTS	L.I.		C.A.P.		Word Test		Reading Test Score	Writing		Hearing Sound in Words	
	54	Stanine	24	Stanine	15	Stanine			Stanine	37	Stanine
Initial test Date:											
Retest Date:											
Further Test (1)											
Further Test (2)											

RECOMMENDATIONS: (for class teacher, or for review, or further teaching, or further assessment)

RESUMEN DE LA OBSERVACIÓN PARA PRUEBAS MÚLTIPLES

Nombre _____

Fecha de Nacimiento _____

Escuela _____

RESUMEN DEL REGISTRO PROGRESIVO

Títulos del Texto	Palabras Actuales Error	Proporción de Errores	Exactitud	Proporción de Autocorrección

Prueba Inicial   Fecha: _____

1. Fácil _____   _____   1: _____   _____%   1: _____

2. Requiere Enseñanza _____   _____   1: _____   _____%   1: _____

3. Difícil _____   _____   1: _____   _____%   1: _____

Repetición de la Prueba   Fecha: _____

1. Fácil _____   _____   1: _____   _____%   1: _____

2. Requiere Enseñanza _____   _____   1: _____   _____%   1: _____

3. Difícil _____   _____   1: _____   _____%   1: _____

Prueba Adicional   Fecha: _____

1. Fácil _____   _____   1: _____   _____%   1: _____

2. Requiere Enseñanza _____   _____   1: _____   _____%   1: _____

3. Difícil _____   _____   1: _____   _____%   1: _____

PRUEBAS	I.L		C.T.I.		Prueba de Palabra		Resultado de la Prueba de Lectura	Escritura		Oír Sonidos en Palabras	
	61	Estanina	25	Estanina	20	Estanina			Estanina	39	Estanina
Prueba inicial Fecha:											
Repetición de prueba Fecha:											
Prueba Adicional (1) Fecha:											
Prueba Adicional (2) Fecha:											

RECOMENDACIONES: (Para el maestro, para revisar, para complementar la enseñanza, o para evaluación adicional).

SECTION IV

CONCLUSIONS AND SUMMARY

9 THE TEACHER AND THE OBSERVATIONS

Kathy Escamilla
with Marie Clay

Clay asserts that the observant teacher must respond sensitively to the individual child's next step into new territory. How can s/he do this?

1 S/he must be familiar with what the child already knows.
2 S/he must be close at hand as s/he reads and writes.
3 S/he must know how to support her/his next leap forward. S/he must allow children enough space to be independent learners.

Such knowledge allows the teacher to guide literacy learning in individual children. The teacher must monitor the progress of individual school entrants; otherwise her program could be holding back the fast movers or dragging along those who approach literacy slowly and cautiously.

A teaching program can be organized so that the teacher

* can observe how children are working and learning
* can make and keep records
* can monitor the progress of the competent children at *spaced* intervals
* and can monitor and guide the teaching of the less competent children at frequent intervals.

In addition, bilingual education teachers must be mindful of the following as they observe the literacy development of two-language children.

* It is preferable that literacy instruction be grounded in the child's native language during early literacy development.
* Effective instruction avoids concurrent translation from English to Spanish or vice versa during early literacy development.
* Code-switching in children is a natural phenomenon when children live in environments where two languages come into contact, but teachers need to work to develop and maintain both language systems.

In view of the above, the teacher must work to create an environment in which literacy in Spanish as well as English is at the center of the instructional program and on the teacher's mind as s/he guides instruction.

THE UTILITY OF OBSERVING READING BEHAVIOR

Running records of text reading can be used whenever oral reading is appropriate. Teachers can use them in many ways, and they are easily used in both Spanish and English.

1 *Capturing behavior for later consideration.* When teachers take a running record as the child reads his/her book they find they notice more about what the child is trying to do. They can also look back over this record, replay in their minds exactly what the children said and did, check on the validity of their assumptions, and think about the behavior. The record captures the behavior of the moment.

2 *Quantifying the record.* If a teacher knows how many words there are in the text that the child reads, s/he can quickly turn this behavior into an accuracy score and relate this to a gradient of book difficulty. For example, unaided the child reads Book Level Seven with 95 percent accuracy but Book Level Eight with 87 percent accuracy.

3 *A cumulative record.* Change over time can be captured with such records taken from time to time during the child's usual reading to the teacher.

4 *Placement.* From such records teachers can place children in groups or classes in a school. A child who is changing her/his school can be quickly checked to see at what level s/he will succeed in a new school.

5 *Critical decisions*. Critical decisions about giving the young child special assistance of some kind, or rapid promotion, or a referral to the school psychologist can be supported with a report on the child's reading behavior on texts from a running record. Clay advised child psychology students to ask for such records (partly because it puts a responsibility on teachers to be observant and partly because it saves the psychologist's time).

6 *Establishing text difficulty*. Clay (1993) thinks of reading progress as being able to read increasingly difficult texts with accuracy and understanding. Running records are used by teachers to try out a child on a book to test the difficulty level of the text in relation to the child's competencies. Having such a behavioral record of exactly how a pupil reads a particular text gives teachers confidence to allow different children to move through different books at different speeds. They know they can still keep track of individual progress.

7 *Observing particular difficulties*. Running records provide opportunities for observing children's confusions and difficulties. The teacher records every correct response with a tick or check mark and records all error and self-correction behavior. This provides evidence of how the child works on words in text, what success s/he has, and what strengths s/he brings to the task. A teacher can quickly decide what might be the next most profitable learning point for that child and can test this out during teaching.

8 *Research purposes*. The records of well-trained teachers taken on a series of texts with a known gradient of difficulty can yield a ranking of students on level by accuracy that will correlate highly with test scores in the first two to three years of schooling. In the case of children learning to read in Spanish, running records can be used to follow students as they progress in Spanish reading and add on English reading in the process of becoming biliterate.

INFORMATION FOR THE EDUCATION SYSTEM

There are several ways that an education system or school system or a cluster of classes in a school can gain information on performance in that system by observing reading behaviors.

1 *Program emphases*. If a supervising teacher takes records of text reading with a wide sample of children s/he will quickly find out if the teaching program is out of balance. Word-by-word reading, spelling out words, not attending to meaning, ignoring the first letter cues or word endings—all these will stand out clearly in the records. And so will the good outcomes—like getting it all together smoothly, working on words in ways that surprise the teacher, enjoying the stories and commenting on possible plot and character outcomes, relating what is being read to other experiences. These types of observations in Spanish/English bilingual programs can be very useful in creating conversations about the quality of Spanish reading instruction and ways to enhance such instruction. Too often, these conversations about literacy in Spanish are not taking place in schools with bilingual programs.

2 *New program features*. If a program is changed and new emphases are introduced, running records can be used to monitor the effects. Do the desired changes in children's processing of texts show up on the records? Do the records suggest any minor adjustments, now, without waiting for the summated assessment at the end of the year?

3 *Running records*. Since running records require the use of real books, they have the added impact of encouraging schools to expand their collections of children's literature in Spanish and encouraging teachers to read and become more familiar with this literature.

4 *Training teachers*. A running record is an assessment which leads the teacher to ask her/himself questions about the child's needs. As s/he takes a record a teacher may discover new behaviors and begin to think about learning in new ways. For example, sometimes the reader goes back, repeating her/himself, rerunning the correct message. Why does s/he do that? S/he was correct. Could it be that the child is surprised by what s/he read and has rerun to monitor her/his own behavior to ensure that it is correct? Monitoring one's own language activities has a great deal of relevance for learning. It is important and needs to be encouraged.

Another contribution to teacher training occurs

when teachers keep today's record as a baseline and over several occasions observe the child again, capturing progress. It is informative to look back at the records of the changes that have occurred.

5   *Information for lay persons.* Two groups that make demands on teachers in the United States as well as New Zealand are parents and administrators. Clay (1993) reports that she has been surprised at how impressed both groups have been with the outcomes of running records taken over time. Teachers have used graphs of the reading progress (see p. 61) of children through their reading books in their appeals for resources to school management committees and school boards. Parents have also been reassured by such records and by sharing with the teacher the folios of work that show the child's progressions in writing. We have found that behavioral records, if thoughtfully planned, communicate clearly to lay persons interested in education. Note that it is not the actual running records that have been shared with lay people. Given the frequent criticism that bilingual programs are not accountable for student progress, running records in Spanish can also be an important means of reporting the student progress to the larger community.

In addition to running records, other observation procedures reported in this early intervention survey in Spanish are Concepts About Print, Spanish Writing Vocabulary, Hearing Sounds in Words (Dictation), and Spanish Letter Identification. These can show teachers which children do not understand some basic concepts about books and print, which children are trying to read with little knowledge of letters, and which ones seem to know words but are not noticing letter sequences within them. The confusions of young readers belong to all beginners: it is just that the successful children sort themselves out and the unsuccessful do not.

To minimize carelessness, bias, and variability in observation records:

- There has to be a gradient of difficulty in the texts used for reading both first and second languages.
- The teachers must be well trained and proficient in both languages.
- Teachers must be similarly trained, so that six teachers scoring the same record would all get the same results; one teacher reading another teacher's record should be able to replay what the child actually said.

INFORMATION TO SUPPORT AN EARLY INTERVENTION FOR SOME CHILDREN

Early identification of children at risk in literacy learning has proved to be possible and should be systematically carried out not later than one year after the child has entered a formal program. This gives the shy and slow children time to settle in and adjust to the demands of a teacher. It also overcomes the problems of trying to identify those who fail to learn to read before some of them have had a chance to learn what reading is about. In many ways it is sensible to try to predict this only after all children have had some equivalent opportunities to respond to good teaching.

Each child will differ in what is confusing, what gaps there are in knowledge and in ways of operating on print. Failing children might respond to an intervention program especially tailored to their needs in one-to-one instruction. Teachers who had found the observation procedures useful for identifying children in need of individual attention have asked Clay for further guidance. How should they teach those failing children? They were asking for specific teaching procedures they felt they were not able to invent.

Most of the assumptions about reading achievement and reading difficulty would not lead us to expect that children who have difficulty would ever catch up to their classmates or make continued normal progress. They would have to learn at greatly accelerated rates of progress to do that. The Reading Recovery development program developed by Clay questioned whether such assumptions were well founded. She asked how many children given a quality intervention early in their schooling could achieve and maintain normal levels of progress. In other words, for what percentage of the children having reading difficulties was it really a question of never having gotten started with appropriate learning patterns?

A quality model of Reading Recovery (see Clay 1993) provides several dimensions of assistance for struggling children in addition to their class program.

- Firstly, a shift to one-to-one instruction allows the teacher to design a program that begins where the child is and not where the curriculum is. Any grouping of children for teaching forces a compromise on this position.
- Then, daily instruction increases the power of the intervention.

- The teacher strives to make the child independent of her/him (to overcome one of the major problems of remedial instruction) and s/he never does for the child anything that s/he can teach him to do for her/himself.
- Acceleration is achieved by all the above means and also because the teacher never wastes valuable learning time or teaching something the child does not need to learn. S/he moves him/her to a harder text as soon as this is feasible but backs such progressions with quantities of easy reading.
- From sound theory of the reading process the child is taught "how to": how to carry out operations to solve problems in text, how to monitor her/his reading, how to check her/his options, how to work independently on print.

It is not enough to have systematic observation procedures that monitor the progress of individual children. To be really effective a powerful second chance program must be provided. It must be viable within the education system, and it must have its own checks and balances to give quality assurance and quality control.

It must live in and adapt to small and large schools, small and large education systems, and differing populations and reading programs. Many interventions for children with special needs never get to consider these issues. It is necessary to demonstrate:

- that the program can work with children
- that teachers can be trained to make it work
- that the program can fit into the organization of the schools
- that it can be run and maintained within an education system.

In considering those issues Clay (1993) has discovered that quality control of an intervention to recover failing children requires teachers who can make sensitive observations in systematic ways, but this is alone not sufficient. It also requires:

- that teachers be trained concurrently in the conceptual and practical aspects of the program
- that they understand the teaching procedures
- that they apply them consistently and critically
- that they can articulate and discuss their assumptions
- that they are supervised for a probationary period
- that those training teachers thoroughly understand the theory on which the program and procedures were based

- that the teacher is a member of a school team that is mounting the intervention to reduce reading difficulties in that school
- that the education system supply resources for early intervention to save a higher outlay later to provide for older children still struggling with literacy.

As *El Instrumento de Observación* detailed in this book was created in Spanish, a model for Reading Recovery in Spanish was also developed. This program, titled *Descubriendo La Lectura*, mirrors the theoretical framework for early intervention originally developed by Clay as well as the intensive and sustained model for the preparation of teachers to work in the program. To date, studies conducted on Spanish-speaking students involved in *Descubriendo La Lectura* have supported many of Clay's findings from Reading Recovery research. Specifically, the results of two studies examining the impact of *Descubriendo La Lectura* on Spanish-speaking students (Escamilla 1992, 1994) have concluded that student acceleration in the Spanish programs occurs in the same way and at the same rate as the English program. Further, the program has proven to have a positive impact on Spanish-speaking students who were inappropriately placed in reading instruction during their first year in school (e.g., Spanish-speaking students who were in all-English kindergarten programs and did not progress because they did not understand the language of instruction), students who are code-switchers (they use English as well as Spanish when they communicate orally), and students who are struggling to become literate for whatever other reasons.

It must be emphasized here that the success of *Descubriendo La Lectura* can be attributed, in part, to the fact that it mirrored the English Reading Recovery Program in breadth and depth. Implementation shortcuts were avoided, and the program was embraced in its entirety by its developers.

AN OVERVIEW

Low achievers cannot profit from group instruction as easily as well-prepared children in the early years of school, so we need to fine-tune our instruction toward their individual learning histories rather than buy another new curriculum or switch to a new method.

Systematic observation allows teachers to go to where the child is and begin teaching from there. Often teachers say that when children get to a point where the program begins they are "ready" for instruction; until then they are "not ready." It makes more sense for the teacher to become a sensitive observer of children during activities so as to help them make the transitions we plan for them.

A year at school will give most children a chance to settle, and to begin to try their abilities in literacy. Systematic observation will uncover which children are forming good or poor strategies, habits, and skills to conceptualize as central to learning at this stage. It makes good psychological and administrative sense to find out early which children are becoming confused by standard educational practices, so that they can be offered alternative approaches to the same goals.

Teachers must monitor the changes that are occurring in the individual learner if they are going to fine-tune their programs. Otherwise they will be holding back the fast movers or dragging along the slow movers already out of their depth. Low achievers can learn quite well if teachers use individual assessments to guide their teaching interactions with a particular child. Teachers need assessments that tell them about the child's existing repertoire and how s/he is getting to those responses, and whether s/he is relating information from one area of competency to another. In literacy learning we are looking at ways of capturing:

- process
- repertoire
- strategies
- problem solving.

We want to record change over time in all these things as the child moves up a gradient of difficulty with increasing independence of teacher support.

If instruction is flexible enough to respect individuality in the first stages of new learning, it can bring children gradually to the point where group instruction can proceed effectively with few confusions.

Observational instruments can arise from theory and can lead to research. A variety of theories may lead to observational tasks: measurement theory, or the psychology of learning, or developmental theory about change over time, or the study of individual differences, or theories of social factors and the influences of contexts on learning. Observational tasks direct teacher attention to the ways in which children are finding sources of information in texts and working with that information.

Typically this approach calls for time with individuals. There is an enormous mental barrier that says, "this is not a teacher's role." Clay says, emphatically, it is!

Teachers can be more effective when they seek and use observational data to inform their teaching. Therefore we need tasks that fit easily into the busy schedule of a teacher's day. If possible we must find good observational appraisals that have *sound measurement characteristics and can be used by the teacher on the run in day-to-day classroom practice.* Such assessments can be compared from one time to the next, from one classroom to the next, and from one school to the next. It is our hope that this book has emphasized that this information is equally as important for two-language children as it is for teachers of children who speak only English.

GLOSARIO DE TÉRMINOS Y FRASES PARA EL PROGRAMA "DESCUBRIENDO DE LA LECTURA"

Accelerate: acelerar

Accumulated writing vocabulary: acumulación del vocabulario de la escritura

Accuracy: exactitud

Appeal: pedir ayuda

Behind the glass: detrás del vidrio

Book introduction: introducción del libro

CAP, Concepts about print: conceptos del texto impreso

Chunk: parte, parte (de una) palabra, trozo, pedazo

Confusions: confusiones

Correspondence: correspondencia, reciprocidad, relación

Cross-check: comprobar, verificar, revisar comparativamente

Cross-checking: hacer una comparación, revisar comparativamente, hacer una comparación, comprobar

Cue: información claves, fuentes de información

Cue source: origen de una clave, fuente de información

Dialogue: diálogo

Dictation: dictado

Directional movement: movimiento direccional

Directionality: orientación direccional

Discontinue: descontinuar, completar del programa

Dismiss: despedir, remover del programa

Easy: fácil, sencillo(a)

Error rate: proporción, porcentaje de errores

Exit: completar del programa

(With) Expression: con expresión

Familiar rereading: lectura conocida o familiar o texto familiar o conocido

Flexible: flexible

Fluency: fluidez

Focus: enfoque (n), enfocar(se) (v)

Frame: (v) poner en cuardro, encuadrar; marca

Frequently: con frecuencia, frecuentemente

Further assessment: más amplia evaluación, evaluación adicional

Further test: prueba (exámen) adicional

Hearing sounds in words task: oír sonidos de las palabras

High self-concept: un buen autoconcepto, tener un autoconcepto bueno

Initial test: prueba (exámen) inicial

Integrate: integrar(se)

Intervention: intervención

Inventing text: invertar el texto, crear el texto

Known words: palabras conocidas o familiares

Lesson: lección

Letter identification (L.I.): identificación de letras

Level: nivel

Link: relacionar(se) a (v), asociar(se), conexión (n), relación (n)

Make and break: hacer y deshacer, formar y separar (palabras)

Minimal introduction: introducción mínima o mínima introducción

More powerful: más fuerte, más potente o intenso

MSV (meaning; structure or syntax, visual):

SEV (significado), estructura o visual

Multiple cues: claves múltiples

Multiple tests: pruebas (exámenes) múltiples

New book: el libro nuevo, texto nuevo

Observation summary for multiple tests: resumen de la observación para pruebas (exámenes) múltiples

Observation survey: instrumento de observación

One-to-one correspondence: pareo de uno a uno/aparear/parear

Orchestrate: orquestar, dirigir, organizar, desarrollar

Point: señalar, apuntar, indicar

Praise: elogiar, halagar

Predict: predecir

Prompt: (v) ar, sugerir, (n) sugerencia

Reading test score: resultados de la prueba (del examen) de lectura

Record: anotación, apunte, archivo, análisis (all nouns)

Reinforce/praise: reforzar, apoyar, animar (see praise)

Reread: leer otra vez, leer una vez más, leer de nuevo

Retest: repetición de la prueba (examen); (n) probar otra vez, tomar una prueba otra vez

Risk taker: ser arriesgado(a), persona que toma riesgos

Roaming in the known: explorar lo conocido o lo familiar

Running record: análisis actual (progresivo) del texto

Running words: palabras actuales (del texto)

Self-correct: autocorregir(se)

Self-correction: autocorrección

Self-esteem: autoestima, autoestimación

Self-monitor: (v) autorevisar, (n) autorevisión

Sesión: período escolar

Spelling: deletreo

Story: cuento, historia, narración

Strategy: estrategia

Summary of running record: resumen del análisis actual (progresivo)

Task: tarea

Test: prueba, examen

Text difficulty: dificultad del texto

Text titles: títulos del texto

Theory: teoría

Transition: transición, cambio

Underline with your finger: subrayar con el dedo

Visual cues: claves visuales

Vocabulary: vocabulario

Word analysis: análisis de las palabras

Word development: desarrollo de las palabras, desarrollar las palabras

Writing sample: muestra, de (la) escritura

Traducción: Lydia Garcia, Traductora del TUSD

REFERENCES AND FURTHER READING

Allington, R., and Broikou, R. 1988. "Development of Shared Knowledge: A New Role for Classroom and Specialist Teachers." *The Reading Teacher* 41:806–21.

Aman, M. G., and Singh, N. M. 1983. "Specific Reading Disorders: Concepts of Etiology Reconsidered." In K. D. Gadow and I. Bader (Eds.), *Advances in Learning and Behavioural Disabilities* 2:1–47. Greenwich, CT: JAI Press.

Ambert, A. 1988. *Bilingual Education and English as a Second Language: A Research Handbook*. New York: Garland.

Barrera, R. B. 1989. *Issues Related to Pullout and Remedial Programs and Student Achievement: A Review of the Research*. Symposium presented at the University of Arizona, October.

Barrera, R. B. 1992. "The Cultural Gap in Literature-based Literacy Instruction." *Education and Urban Society* 24:227–43.

Brena, D. 1995. *The Descubriendo La Lectura Early Intervention Reading Program: A Case Study of One Student's Progress from Spanish to English*. Paper presented at the Reading Recovery Annual Conference, Columbus, Ohio.

Brena, D., and García, A. 1993. *Language Variation Among Mexican-American, Puerto Rican and Cuban-American Children Taking El Instrumento de Observación*. Paper presented at the Reading Recovery Annual Meeting, Columbus, Ohio.

Brigance Diagnostic Assessment of Basic Skills: Word Recognition Section (Spanish Version). 1984. North Billerica, MA: Curriculum Associates.

Brown, A. 1992. "Building Community Support Through Local Educational Funds." *NABE News* 15:4–5.

Brown, R. A. 1973. *A First Language: The Early Stages*. Cambridge: Harvard University Press.

Bruner, J. S. 1990. *Acts of Meaning*. Cambridge, MA: Harvard University Press.

Cazden, C. B. 1988. *Classroom Discourse: The Language of Teaching*. Portsmouth, NH: Heinemann.

Clay, M. M. 1966. *Emergent Reading Behavior*. Unpublished doctoral dissertation, University of Auckland Library.

———. 1972. *Sand*. Auckland, New Zealand: Heinemann.

———. 1979a. *Reading: The Patterning of Complex Behaviour* (2d ed.). Auckland, New Zealand: Heinemann.

———. 1979–1986. *The Early Detection of Reading Difficulties* (3d ed.). Auckland, New Zealand: Heinemann.

———. 1979b. *Stones*. Auckland, New Zealand: Heinemann.

———. 1982. *Observing Young Readers: Selected Papers*. Portsmouth, NH: Heinemann.

———. 1989. "Concepts About Print: In English and Other Languages." *The Reading Teacher* 42 (4):268–77.

———. 1991. *Becoming Literate: The Construction of Inner Control*. Auckland, New Zealand: Heinemann.

———. 1993a. *Reading Recovery: A Guidebook for Teachers in Training*. Auckland, New Zealand: Heinemann.

———. 1993b. *An Observation Survey of Early Literacy Achievement*. Portsmouth, NH: Heinemann.

Clay M. M., and Imlach, R. H. 1971. "Juncture, Pitch, and Stress As Reading Behaviour Variables." *Journal of Verbal Behaviour and Verbal Learning* 10:133–39.

Commins, N., and Miramontes, O. 1989. "Perceived and Actual Linguistic Competence: A Descriptive Study of Four Low-achieving Hispanic Bilingual Students." *American Education Research Journal* 26:443–72.

Cornejo, R. 1980. *Cornejo's Spanish Word Frequency List*. Paper presented at the annual conference of the National Association for Bilingual Education, Anaheim, CA.

Cowley, J. 1986. *Nuestra Abuelita*. San Diego, CA: The Wright Group.

Cummins, J. 1989. *Empowering Minority Students*. Sacramento, CA: California Association for Bilingual Education.

Department of Education. 1985. *Reading in the Junior Classes*. Wellington: Learning Media.

Escamilla, K. 1987. *The Relationship of Native Language Reading Achievement and Oral English Proficiency to Future Achievement in Reading English As a Second Language*. Unpublished doctoral dissertation, University of California, Los Angeles.

————. 1992a. *Descubriendo La Lectura: An Application of Reading Recovery in Spanish*. Report prepared for the office of Educational Research and Improvement (OERI) from a grant provided by the OERI Fellows Program, 1991–92. Washington, D.C.

————. 1992b. "Theory to Practice: A Look at Maintenance Bilingual Education Classrooms." *The Journal of Educational Issues of Language Minority Students* 11: 1–23

————. 1994. "The Sociolinguistic Environment of a Bilingual School: A Case Study." *Bilingual Research Journal* 18 (1)(2):21–47.

Escamilla, K., and Andrade, A. 1992. "Descubriendo La Lectura: An Application of Reading Recovery in Spanish." *Education and Urban Society* 24 (2):212–26.

Escamilla, K.; Basurto, A.; Andrade; and Ruíz, O. 1992. *Descubriendo La Lectura: A Study of Methods of Assessing and Identifying the Reading Needs of Spanish-Speaking First Grade Students*. Paper presented at the National Association for Bilingual Education Conference (NABE), Albuquerque, NM.

Ferdman, B. 1990. "Literacy and cultural identity." *Harvard Education Review*, 60:181–204.

Fernald, G. M. 1943. *Remedial Techniques in Basic School Subjects*. New York: McGraw-Hill.

Ferreiro, E., and Teberosky, A. 1982. *Literacy Before Schooling*. Portsmouth, NH: Heinemann.

Fradd, S., and Tikunoff, W. 1987. *Bilingual Education and Bilingual Special Education: A Guide for Administrators*. Boston: College Hill.

Genishi, C. 1982. "Observational Research Methods for Early Childhood Education." In B. Spodek (Ed.) *Handbook of Research in Early Childhood Education*. New York: The Free Press.

Giroux, H. 1985. Theories of Reproduction and Resistance in the New Sociology of Education: A critical analysis. *Harvard Education Review* 55 (5):257–93.

Goodman, Y. M., and Burke, C. 1972. *The Reading Miscue Inventory*. New York: Macmillan.

Hakuta, K., and Gould, S. 1987. "Synthesis of Research on Bilingual Education." *Education Leadership* 44 (6):38–45.

Hornberger, N. H. 1992. "Bi-literacy Contents, Continua, and Contrasts: Policy and Curriculum for Cambodian and Puerto Rican Students in Philadelphia." *Education and Urban Society* 24:196–211.

Johns, J. L. 1980. "First graders' Concepts About Print." *Reading Research Quarterly* 15 (4):529–49.

Johnston, P. H. 1992. *Constructive Evaluation of Literate Activity*. New York: Longman.

Krashen, S., and Biber, D. 1988. *On course: Bilingual Education's Success in California*. Sacramento: California Association for Bilingual Education.

Lyman, H. B. 1963. *Test Scores and What They Mean*. Englewood Cliffs, NJ: Prentice Hall.

Lyons, J. May 1991. "The View from Washington." *NABE News* 14 (5):1.

McKenzie, M. 1989. *Journeys into Literacy*. Huddersfield: Schofield and Sims.

Medina, M., Jr., and Escamilla, K. 1992a. "English Acquisition by Fluent- and Limited-Spanish-Proficient Mexican Americans in a Three-Year Maintenance Bilingual Program." *Hispanic Journal of Behavioral Sciences* 14 (2):252–67.

————. 1992b. "Evaluation of Transitional and Maintenance Bilingual Programs." *Urban Education* 27 (3):263–90.

————. 1993. "English and Spanish Acquisition by Limited-Language-Proficient Mexican Americans in a Three-Year Maintenance Bilingual Program." *Hispanic Journal of Behavioral Services* 15 (1):108–20.

Modiano, N. 1968. "National or Mother Tongue in Beginning Reading: A Comparative Study." *Research in the Teaching of English*, II (I): 32–43.

Morrow, L. M. 1989. *Literacy Development in the Early Years: Helping Children Read and Write*. Englewood Cliffs, NJ: Prentice Hall.

Neale, M. D. 1958. *The Neale Analysis of Reading Ability*. London: Macmillan. ACER, 1988. NFER-Nelson, 1989.

Paley, V. 1981. *Wally's Stories*. Cambridge, MA: Harvard University Press.

Ramírez, D. J., Yuen, S. D., and Ramey, D. R. 1991. *Executive Summary, Final Report: Longitudinal Study of Structured English Immersion Strategy, Early-Exit and Late-Exit Transitional Bilingual Education Programs for Language-Minority Children*

(Contract No. 300-87-0156). San Mateo, CA: Aguirre International.

Robinson, S. M. 1973. *Predicting Early Reading Progress.* Unpublished master's thesis, University of Auckland Library.

Rodríguez, A. 1988. "Research in Reading and Writing in Bilingual Education and English as a Second Language." In A. Ambert (Ed.) *Bilingual Education and English as a Second Language: A Research Handbook.* New York: Garland.

Santillana Basal Spanish Reading Program. 1984. Los Angeles, CA: Santillana.

Shannon, S. 1995. "The Bilingual Classroom as a Site of Resistance to the Hegemony of English." *Urban Review.*

Skutnabb-Kangas, T. 1981. *Bilingualism or Not: The Education of Minorities.* Clevedon, Avon: Multilingual Matters.

Smith, F. 1978. *Understanding Reading* (2d ed.). New York: Holt, Rinehart and Winston.

Stallman, A. C., and Pearson, P. D. 1990. "Formal Measures of Early Literacy." In L. M. Morrow and J. K. Smith (Eds.), *Assessment for Instruction in Early Literacy.* Englewood Cliffs, NJ: Prentice Hall.

Thonis, E. 1981. *Reading Instruction for Language Minority Students. Schooling and Language Minority Students: A Theoretical Framework.* Los Angeles, CA: Evaluation, Dissemination and Assessment Center, California State University, Los Angeles.

Troike, R. 1978. *Research Evidence for the Effectiveness of Bilingual Education.* Bilingual Education Paper Series, 2 (5). Los Angeles, CA: Evaluation, Dissemination and Assessment Center, California State University, Los Angeles.

Wells, G. 1986. *The Meaning Makers: Children Learning Language and Using Language to Learn.* Portsmouth, NH: Heinemann.

Whitmore, K., and Andrade, R. 1989. *Semilingualism: An Institutional Model for Pedagogy.* Paper presented at the Second Annual Language, Reading, and Culture Colloquy, University of Arizona, Tucson.

Willig, A. 1985. "A Meta-analysis of Selected Studies on Effectiveness of Bilingual Education." *Review of Educational Research* 55:269–317.

INDEX